Jeremy Duff is the Direct
Diocese and a canon of Liv
New Testament and Greek i

Joanna Collicutt McGrath v   ......ant clinical neuropsychologist, spec........g in the area of rehabilitation
and complex disability. She has also studied theology, and has a
special interest in the relationship between psychology, health care
and theology. She is an Anglican deacon.

MEETING JESUS

Human Responses to a Yearning God

Jeremy Duff
and
Joanna Collicutt McGrath

First published in Great Britain in 2006

Society for Promoting Christian Knowledge
36 Causton Street
London SW1P 4ST

British Library Cataloguing-in-Publication Data
A catalogue record for this book is available from the British Library

ISBN-13: 978–0–281–05707–8
ISBN-10: 0–281–05707–9

1 3 5 7 9 10 8 6 4 2

Typeset by Graphicraft Ltd, Hong Kong
Printed in Great Britain by Bookmarque Ltd, Croydon, Surrey

For our parents: John and Stella, Sid and Jenny

Contents

re p 35:
parables) — 1) The Lost Son
                    2) The searching woman and
                          lost coin
                    3) The lost son
            — The dishonest manager

Preface

This book is about meeting and journeying. It is about Jesus as he is presented to us in the Gospel of Luke. Through Luke's narrative we meet the Jesus who journeyed around Galilee meeting people, telling parables that spoke of their human yearnings and of the God who was searching for them.

Our experience in writing this book was that the boundaries of past and present dissolved as we examined the thoughts, attitudes and actions – the psychology – of those depicted. Our hope is that this will also be the experience of our readers. For our own human yearnings are in fact very similar to those of the people whom Jesus met, and the characters in the stories he told. Luke could have been writing about us, so it is perhaps not surprising that through reading and reflecting in depth on his text we can find ourselves meeting afresh with Jesus, and grasping more clearly the nature of the searching God. Our hope is that this book will contribute to the process of reflecting, journeying, and meeting.

Meeting and journeying were also central in the development of the book itself. It is the product of the repeated meeting and journeying together of its two authors. We come from different directions – one with a background in New Testament scholarship, the other with a background in clinical neuropsychology, one a man, the other a woman – bringing with us our complementary expertise and perspectives, unified in a passion to take seriously both the text of the Gospel, and the reality of human life. However, this book is not just the result of a meeting. We journeyed together for two years, wrestling with the meaning and implications of these texts from Luke's Gospel. The result is a jointly authored text. No part of the text originates from only one of the authors – indeed, for large parts of it we can ourselves no longer remember who wrote which words. This process has been greatly illuminating, if also trying at times, for both of us. We have learnt from each other, and we hope from God, as we have written this book together. We believe that the result has a richness beyond what either of us individually could have achieved.

We have tried to strike a balance in the provision of notes. We want to help readers follow up ideas that we raise, without the book becoming overburdened with footnotes and other scholarly apparatus. Within each chapter there are a few notes indicating the sources of quotations, or a starting point for pursuing an idea. The 'Further reading' section at the end of the book gives a categorized list of books that we would recommend for those who wish to take things further.

Luke's Gospel was written in Greek not English and yet for the readers' sake we wished to present the text, and quotations from elsewhere in the Bible, in English. Translation is not a neutral exercise though – it always involves interpretation. Therefore we have presented our own translations of the text in keeping with the interpretation presented. The translation is, in effect, the result of our exegetical work, not the beginning. However, the reader will find that only rarely is there a notable difference from the text given in most modern Bible translations. In such cases, the text of the chapter will contain a discussion justifying and explaining the translation presented.

We have not journeyed alone. Both of us are conscious that the ideas contained in this book have their roots in many conversations and encounters with colleagues, teachers and students over the years. More directly, we would want to mention Alison Barr, Andrew Briggs, Jill Duff, Jane Durham, Rod Garner, Alister McGrath, Bob Morgan, Martyn Payne, Stefan Schuller, Peter Walker and Henry Wansbrough, and thank them for the various ways in which they contributed to this book. However, this does not at all imply that they would agree with everything in the book, and any errors are our own. Particular thanks are due to Valerie Fisher, the warden of Chester Retreat House, where this book took its final shape.

1

A meeting with Jesus

Jesus arrived at Jericho and was passing through it. Now there was a man there called Zacchaeus who was a senior tax collector and was rich. *He was trying to see who Jesus was*, yet couldn't because of the crowd, for he was small. So he ran on ahead and climbed up into a sycamore tree which Jesus was going to pass by, so that he could see him. When Jesus reached the spot, *he looked up* and said to him, 'Zacchaeus, quick, get down, for I must stay at your house today.' He hurried down and happily welcomed him. Now everyone who saw this began to grumble, complaining that he had gone to be the guest of a sinner. Zacchaeus stopped and said to the Lord, 'Half of my possessions, Lord, I will give to the poor; and if I have cheated anyone of anything, I will pay it back four times over.' Jesus said to him, 'Today salvation has come to this house, because this man is also a son of Abraham. *For the Son of Man has come to seek out, and save, the lost.* (*Luke 19.1–10*)

There is so much in Luke's account of this meeting between two people. In the short space of ten verses it touches on key theological and psychological themes that we shall explore in depth in this book. But what this story tells us at its most fundamental is that the encounter between God and humanity, which seems to be the goal of human searching, spiritual journey or pilgrimage, is equally the end point of a process of divine seeking. Zacchaeus thought he was looking for Jesus, but Jesus was also looking for Zacchaeus. Furthermore, Zacchaeus' initial role in this episode was that of spectator but, at the invitation of Jesus, he became an actor or participant. He achieved his goal of seeing Jesus visually by climbing the tree, but he only achieved his goal of seeing 'who Jesus was' by becoming involved with Jesus, by a genuine meeting with him that culminated in his welcoming him into his home.

1

Zacchaeus was looking over the shoulders of other people through physical necessity, social exclusion and embarrassment. As we read of the meetings between Jesus and people in the Gospels we too are looking over shoulders, distant as we are in time and place from the original events. Yet our need to be drawn into the action, to experience our own authentic encounter with Jesus, is as pressing now as it was for Zacchaeus two thousand years ago.

Above all else Christianity is about Jesus. What it says about Jesus can be put in many different ways – who Jesus was or is, what he achieved, how one can relate to him, what he wants for us. Nevertheless, despite these different perspectives and approaches, Jesus remains the focus. For Christianity he is 'the beginning and the end' (Revelation 22.13). This is true not just in the abstract world of theological thinking. For the Christian believer, the journey of faith begins, as it did for Zacchaeus, in an encounter with and response to Jesus. The character of these 'encounters' varies considerably. They can range from an abrupt confrontation (as on the road to Damascus) to a gradual awakening to his presence (as on the road to Emmaus). Sometimes there is an experience so real and dramatic that it can be described in terms of a direct meeting. Other encounters with Jesus are more subtle, and mediated perhaps through the life of other Christians, through the words of the Gospels, through worship or through religious art. Few begin their Christian life without some sense of a spiritual experience of this sort. An encounter with Jesus, and a response to him, is the beginning. Christianity also teaches that an encounter with Jesus will be the end. This is portrayed in different ways – the Son of Man returning (Mark 13.26), a meeting with the Lord (1 Thessalonians 4.17), a final judgement at which those whom Jesus knows will sit and feast with him (Luke 13.28, 29; 23.42, 43), a rising to share his glory (1 Corinthians 15.22, 23, 35–41), living in the New Jerusalem in the light and presence of the Lamb (Revelation 22.3–5). Central to all these expressions of Christian hope is the idea that the climax of the journey of faith, whose beginning was a meeting with Jesus, will be another meeting with Jesus.

The earliest Christian expression of this hope is the Aramaic phrase 'Marana tha' (Our Lord, come!), presumably originating in the Palestinian church, and probably used in the context of worship or as a greeting. This phrase was clearly well established and in widespread use by the time Paul quoted it in his letter to the Gentile church at Corinth written around 55 AD (1 Corinthians 16.22). It indicates a deep yearning for the return of Jesus that can be detected at several points in the New Testament. Its continued use would have both expressed a prevalent need or wish and also maintained a sense of expectation.

Why were these very first Christians so excited about meeting Jesus again? One response to this question among scholars is that times were tough, and that, like many persecuted and marginalized minority groups, Christians longed for an escape to Utopia, together with a vindication of their beliefs and practices. Jesus had promised that he would return. If he did not come then all that they had believed about him, and the coming of God's kingdom on earth, would turn out to be fantasy rather than reality. There is undoubtedly some truth in this analysis. Indeed some scholars hold that Luke's main agenda in writing his Gospel was to help the first Christians come to terms with the fact that Jesus did not return as soon as had been expected. On the other hand, many others argue against this view, pointing out that there is little hard evidence that the 'delay' of Jesus' return actually constituted a significant problem for the early Church.[1]

However, these sorts of arguments miss a crucial point, evident in a sensitive reading of much of the New Testament material. The very earliest Palestinian Christians remembered what it was like to know Jesus the first time around. They were bereaved. They simply missed him and longed to see him again. A sense of what Jesus meant to them is gained from the accounts of their terrible grief at his loss, the need for comfort evident in the final discourses in John's Gospel, and the overwhelming joy of the short-lived reunion with him after the resurrection (see for example Luke 24.14; John 20.21; 16.16–24). This is one way that we know what the earthly Jesus was like. He was not just admired, respected and revered; he was deeply loved by his followers. When you lose someone you love, the hope of a reunion is one of the things that may keep you going. This is well illustrated by Colin

Murray Parkes' comments on the bereavement experience of C. S. Lewis: 'The suspense . . . would seem to indicate the expectation that something is about to happen. To the griever the only happening that seems important is the return of the one who is lost.'[2] The first reunion with Jesus had given his followers both a firm hope that a final reunion could take place, and a taste of the bliss that would go along with it.

As the gospel spread, people who had never met the earthly Jesus came to faith (John 20.29; 1 Peter 1.8), and this coming to faith was not primarily about assenting to a set of theological beliefs and ethical practices. It continued to be defined by an initial encounter and a developing relationship with Jesus, now experienced through the Spirit as the risen Jesus Christ (see for example Ephesians 3.18, 19; Philippians 3.8; 2 Timothy 1.12). Of course the ministry of the early Church involved transmitting the teachings of Jesus, and the development and teaching of a theology about Jesus. What is less obvious, but of key importance, is that it also involved the fostering of *encounter* with Jesus.

One important way that this was achieved was through worship. While there was a tradition that when Christians simply met together Jesus was with them (Matthew 18.20), the Eucharist was from the earliest times a special focus for connecting worshippers with the real events of Jesus' life and death on this earth, and a foretaste of the heavenly feast that would take place when he returned. Paul's first letter to the Corinthians indicates not only that the Eucharist was central to worship in Pauline churches in the 50s AD, but also that the words of institution had been received by Paul as part of an existing tradition (1 Corinthians 11.23–6). In verse 26 Paul explicitly connects the re-enactment of these actions of Jesus with his future coming. The same link is present in all three synoptic gospel accounts of the last supper (Matthew 26.29; Mark 14.25; Luke 22.18).

A second major way that this encounter was fostered is evident in the emergence of a new literary genre, the *gospel*. (The Greek word is *euangelion*, which one might normally translate as 'good news'. The first words in Mark – generally agreed to be the earliest of the four canonical Gospels to be written – are, 'The beginning of the *euangelion* (good news) . . .'.) From the beginning Christians told stories about Jesus and remembered his words, but within little more than a century this remembrance was primarily exercised through the reading of written *gospels*. These were produced in the form of easily portable books rather than the more conventional scrolls, and were thus suitable for both communal worship and private devotion. Their importance in the life of the Church is demonstrated by the development of the canon during the first four centuries AD: long before the shape of the New Testament was finally fixed, the prime position of the four Gospels within it had become unassailable.[3]

It is very hard to pigeonhole these four Gospels. They aren't historical biographies by modern standards, though they do have similarities with some biographies from the ancient world.[4] In terms of their form, they have been described as a series of rather loosely connected episodes of different sorts (stories climaxing in a pronouncement, miracle stories, parables and so on), followed by an extended and more coherent passion narrative. Our familiarity with these gospel-texts and their central place in the New Testament can blind us to the questions they raise. Why was the memory of Jesus preserved in this way? And why did the Church see fit to place no less than four of them right at the beginning of the New Testament? It would be logical to suppose that if Jesus had died, risen and was seated at the right hand of God in heaven, details of his earthly life would no longer have been of central importance to the life of the Church. But clearly they were.

One might argue that details of Jesus' teaching remained important. Presenting these as spoken by Jesus in didactic form such as the Sermon on the Mount, or in dialogue form such as some of the discourses in John's Gospel, would underline their authority and ensure their continued preservation. And indeed there are gospels dating from relatively early times, such as the Gospel of Thomas,[5] that present what they claim to be Jesus' teaching in these ways, but they did not find their way into the New Testament. We will never know for certain all the factors, theological and socio-historical, that led to the pre-eminence of the four Gospels we know today. But we do know what makes them distinct from some of the other gospel-like material that was circulating at the time. The canonical Gospels are distinguished by setting moral teaching and theology firmly in the context of a *narrative of the life, death and resurrection of Jesus.* And these events are characterized by *meetings between Jesus and all sorts of people.*

In 1989 Rowan Williams published an essay that reflected on this phenomenon. He argued that the Gospels we know today were not included in the New Testament under the direction of some central orthodox ecclesiastical committee that had a particular theological agenda. (Thus he responded in anticipation to the assertions made by Dan Brown in his book *The Da Vinci Code.*[6]) Rather, they survived and were revered because they had been found to be a reliable foundation for Christian spirituality over the previous centuries. It follows from his argument that, analogous to the way the biological evolutionary process can be seen as part of God's creative activity, the canonical Gospels can be seen as an example of survival of the fittest. Their job was to nourish the Church. They were superbly fit for this job, and that is why they 'survived'.

The gospel genre offers a chance of meeting with Jesus to those who never met him historically. This is not a meeting with the historical human Jesus, but it is strongly connected with those first person-to-person encounters, connecting the risen and exalted Lord with the Jesus of history. To quote Williams, it is

> . . . a mode . . . which brings the hearer into 'dramatic' relation with the subject of the story – offering the hearer a new self-definition determined by his or her stance towards Jesus . . . the narrative past speaks to the present . . . the transforming encounter with Christ is renewed and deepened by the repeated hearing of the story . . .[7]

Williams both affirms that the Gospels present an essentially historical account of the life, death and resurrection of Jesus, and argues that they do much more than this. Thus, the present encounter and the link with the past are both important. The meeting of the believer with Jesus is not just a spiritual trip, with the dangers of personal wish-fulfilment and the limitations of local

culture and present world-view that this entails. It can be grounded in and verified against the realities of his life story. In meeting
Jesus we are not encountering a *personified* theological idea or
psychological wish but, through the medium of the Gospels, a
remembered historical *person*.[8] So, the Gospels both give us evidence of the continuing importance of meeting with Jesus, and
provide a means by which this may be achieved.

An authentic meeting with Jesus is clearly important in the
process of initial conversion. But it is also vital for the ongoing
Christian life. Jesus is more than the beginning and end – he is also
the Way (John 14.6). Jesus' words in John's Gospel make it clear
that he has not only opened up the way to God (Hebrews 10.20),
that he has not only gone that way ahead of us (Hebrews 2.10;
12.2) but that he is also the Way itself. In walking the Christian way
we follow him, remembering the past by walking the way of the
cross (Luke 9.23) and looking ahead as we walk in newness of
life. Through the Spirit, we also experience him by our side (John
14.25–6; 16.13–14). Most mysterious of all, we find that we are
walking into him, a phenomenon that is acted out in baptism by
immersion (Romans 6.3–11).

This journey of faith is punctuated by moments or periods of re-
encounter with Jesus. Few people claim to live continuously aware
of Jesus' presence with them. On the contrary life is experienced
as a cycle of ebbs and flows, periods of seeming separation from
Jesus, or at least little sense of intimacy or closeness, punctuated
by moments or seasons of close relationship and interaction – that
is times of re-encounter. These meetings with Jesus, meetings of
discovery and rediscovery, are a feature of the ongoing walk. Like
the resurrection encounters for the first Christians, they are both
reminders of our first meeting and tasters of our final meeting.

As we read the gospel stories, we see before us people meeting
with Jesus – we can see their different motives, the different
responses they make, the way in which Jesus acts towards them
and reveals his Father's heart. More than this, though, Christian
experience throughout the millennia is that as we overhear the
gospels' stories of other people's encounters with Jesus, we too
meet Jesus in a new way. We can do more than just read the

story. Like Zacchaeus, we can enter the story and hear Jesus speaking to us. As we meet Jesus afresh in the Gospels we are reminded of 'where we came in'. For us this is a reiteration of our first encounter with Jesus. But it is also a sort of re-living of the encounters of the people in the gospel stories and the encounters of Christians over the centuries with the person of Jesus. So, in connecting with Jesus in this way, we are also making connections with other Christians, we are participating in the body of Christ.

The aim of this book is to foster authentic encounter with the Jesus of the Gospels, by exploring what Luke has to say about the theology and psychology of God's meeting with human beings in his Son. We hope that readers will both deepen their own faith, through reflection on what it means to meet with Jesus and, like Andrew (John 1.42), be encouraged to introduce others to him. The gospel accounts of Jesus' meetings with people work at both a theological and psychological level. This is because they tell of meetings between the human and the divine, between the Son of God and specific human beings. They have an eternal theological meaning but are played out in the world of human thoughts, feelings, actions and relationships – the stuff of psychology. The meeting between Jesus and Zacchaeus quoted at the beginning of this chapter illustrates this well. It contains a complex interweaving of psychological and theological themes, dealing in concentrated form with mutual searching, social exclusion and stigma, the urgent time-frame, the joy of the eschatological feast, forgiveness and envy, repentance and behaviour change, social justice, personal affirmation, Jewish identity and the meaning of salvation. We will return repeatedly to the story of Zacchaeus and develop some of these themes throughout this book.

We have chosen the Gospel of Luke because it is particularly helpful in unpacking these sorts of themes. For a start, Luke is a Gospel about the timing of decision. To use a technical term, Luke has a clear *eschatological* viewpoint. Eschatology literally means the study of the 'end' or the 'last things'. It is concerned with a point of change rather than periods of stability. The eschatology of Jesus had two distinctive features, both drawn out particularly clearly by Luke.

First, Luke tells us that Jesus' message is that God is meeting with his people *now*. People are faced with the need to decide, to take advantage of a limited window of opportunity. The climactic moment is upon them, the kingdom of God is among them, they must read the signs of the times, they must recognize the time of their visitation from God. In some ways this would not have been such a remarkable message in first-century Galilee. John the Baptist was also preaching something of this sort (Luke 3.7–9). Each generation thinks it is living in extraordinary and troubled times, perhaps even living in the last days (Luke 21.9). What made Jesus' approach really distinctive was his *attitude* to the coming of the kingdom of God. He said it was *good* news!

Jesus would have been well aware of the dreadful imagery available in his culture to depict the coming of God in judgement on his people (see for instance Zephaniah 1.14–18). Indeed at times he made use of this imagery himself. Yet the constant thrust of his message was that this day was to be welcomed rather than feared (Luke 9.54), and his principal image for talking about it was of a marvellous party rather than a consuming fire. In Luke's Gospel Jesus' ministry begins with his 'manifesto' presented in Nazareth (Luke 4.16–21), and the Old Testament image which predominates then and throughout this Gospel is that of the day of the Lord's *favour* – the jubilee year of Leviticus 25.10 in which debts were forgiven, and everyone had a new start. Luke emphasizes both this positive emphasis of Jesus' message and its urgency.

The other side of this coin is that for us there are also defining or 'eschatological' moments, marked by a turning towards or away from the God who wants to meet us in Jesus. Like the coming of God's kingdom, the beginning of our journey of faith can be fixed in time and space (to the exact minute for some, more broadly for others). Luke's Gospel pays equal attention to this other side of the coin – to human eschatological moments. This can be seen, for example, in the episode of the repentant thief on the cross, who turns to Jesus in the last moments of his life (Luke 23.39–43). In Luke's Gospel then, the timing of God's action in meeting with his people in Jesus and the timing of human response are both important. Luke also takes great care to stress that the kingdom

9

of God, while a new creation, is also in clear continuity with its Jewish heritage. We see this, for instance, in the description of Zacchaeus as a 'son of Abraham'. In the same way the new creation that is the Christian is a person whose identity is being transformed but who, like the risen Christ on the road to Emmaus (Luke 24.16, 30–1), is still familiar and recognizable.

Following on from this, in Luke's Gospel the psychology of conversion is as important as the eschatology.[9] The process of human decision-making and behaviour change is of as much interest as the timing of the decision. (Later in this book we shall also explore the idea of the 'psychology' of God.) Luke's Gospel is told from the point of view of individuals, whose motives and thought processes are often made explicit. Luke writes with a human psychological interest that goes beyond that of the other gospel writers. In this Gospel we encounter real people, acting in ways with which we can identify, and which lead us on into revealing self-reflection as we ponder the degree to which our lives, thoughts and attitudes match those of the characters portrayed. Luke has depicted in his Gospel a message for all times, and for our times: moments of decision come, when they do they cannot be ignored, and, as in the case of Zacchaeus, their effects echo throughout the rest of our lives.

Finally, and perhaps most importantly, Luke's Gospel contains at its centre a sustained piece of Jesus' teaching about the meeting between God and humankind, a sort of commentary on the events of his own life. This can be found in Chapters 15 and 16, and will form the focus of this book. We understand Luke 15.3–16.13 to be a single thematic piece of teaching, a metaphorical exposition and explanation of Luke 15.1–2. It is followed by a pronouncement or summary statement (Luke 16.14–17), which upholds both the Jewish law and the radical behaviour of Jesus.

Chapter 15 begins with 'The tax collectors and the sinners were drawing near to listen to him'. We accompany this crowd of hopefuls, people like Zacchaeus, wanting to be close to Jesus. There are others present though, the Pharisees and scribes, who grumble at these potential encounters, just as people grumbled about Zacchaeus. They believe Jesus ought to remain separate. This section of teaching closes at Chapter 16 verses 16–17, with Jesus seeming to favour the tax collectors and the sinners. It is they who, despite all their moral ambiguity, are pressing in to meet Jesus. They are the ones who are exerting the effort to enter the kingdom of God; 'forcing' their way in. At the same time Jesus also declares his agreement with the Pharisees' key concern: the law, God's requirements, can never be simply put aside. In this way the radically new nature of the kingdom of God is presented as in continuity with the ancient heritage of Israel. As we have already noted, this deep paradox pervades Luke's Gospel, and is also a dominant concern of the New Testament.

In between the first comments of the Pharisees and scribes and Jesus' pronouncement about the kingdom of God and the law, come four parables: 'The lost sheep', 'The lost coin', 'The lost son' and 'The dishonest manager'. Each deals with the lost and the found, the seekers and the sought. These parables at once make a general theological point about redemption, and at the same time explain what is going on in the rest of the Gospel when Jesus meets specific people like Zacchaeus. (Conversely, the meetings of Jesus with real people can be seen as 'worked examples' of the theology underpinning the parables.) Each parable speaks about how a person comes to encounter God, but each of them is different. In these four stories the inner workings of human hearts and indeed of the divine heart are explored. For they each describe the events surrounding this meeting from a different perspective. In some we see God's perspective in yearning for and seeking out human beings. We see others from the perspective of the human turning back to God. In one the moment of decision is reached rapidly in response to pressing events, in another it is arrived at more slowly in response to a growing sense that there must be a better way. Divine seeking and human turning are the steps that culminate in the encounter (Luke 15.20), placed right at the centre of these four parables. This encounter involves being loved, accepted and held or embraced by God in Jesus. And it is only then, in the context of that meeting that, exactly as in the story of Zacchaeus, human behaviour really changes. Taken together these parables portray what is involved in human encounter with God. In telling these parables Jesus is commentating on, explaining and defending his own behaviour, which is in complete conformity to that of his Father.

Enough of introductions. We invite you to come with us into the centre of Luke's Gospel. Together we will hear some of the stories that Jesus told about God's meeting with humanity. We will ponder the ways in which the human reactions and responses, joys and fears, presented to us, mirror the ways in which we relate to God, and help us to understand the way God relates to us. As we study them, we are in fact studying ourselves. As we watch Jesus meeting people like Zacchaeus, maybe we too will experience a fresh meeting with our Lord.

> Father of all,
> we give you thanks and praise,
> that when we were still far off
> you met us in your Son and brought us home.
> Dying and living, he declared your love,
> gave us grace, and opened the gate of glory.
> May we who share Christ's body live his risen life;
> we who drink his cup bring life to others;
> we whom the Spirit lights give light to the world.
> Keep us firm in the hope you have set before us,
> so we and all your children shall be free,
> and the whole earth live to praise your name;
> through Christ our Lord.
> Amen.

2

Drawing near

———◆◆◆———

All the tax collectors and sinners used to draw near to listen to him.
And the Pharisees and the scribes would complain – 'This man
welcomes sinners and eats with them!'   (*Luke 15.1–2*)

These two short sentences introduce the four parables of Jesus at
the heart of this book. In order to engage with them we first need
to 'draw near' – to enter into their context. Setting the context is
important. These parables are not just strung together randomly,
as a collection of free-floating sayings for us to make of them
what we will. They are thematically linked, and come together in a
particular situation: that of an ongoing argument between Jesus
and certain religious leaders, as Jesus travels throughout towns
and villages 'on the way' from Galilee to Jerusalem.

This sense of an 'ongoing argument' and an 'ongoing journey'
is important, because the tense in the Greek of Luke 15.1 implies
that this is a repeated situation, not a one-off event. This is not
an account of a particular occasion when Jesus' association with
tax collectors and sinners attracted criticism. Luke does, of course,
recount several such occasions, not least the encounter with
Zacchaeus, as we have seen. But here he presents to us a summary
of this distinctive aspect of Jesus' life and teaching, of the disputes
it caused with the Pharisees, and of how he responded to their
complaints. As Jesus journeyed, this is what kept on happening. If
we are to understand these parables, we must first understand
something of this context: the journey and the argument.

The journey

The long central section of Luke's Gospel, beginning at 9.51 and stretching to 19.28, is sometimes referred to as the 'travel narrative'. This is a rather misleading expression because it calls up an image of Jesus as a sort of roving reporter for a television holiday show. Yet Jesus is not a tourist travelling to see the sights, he is on a deliberate journey from his homeland in the northern territory of Galilee to the holy city of Jerusalem in Judea. This is very clearly signalled. The journey begins after the transfiguration, where Jesus' mission is spoken of as being fulfilled at Jerusalem (Luke 9.31). The journey itself begins at 9.51, 'When the time for him to be taken up drew close, he set his face to go to Jerusalem.' The chapters which follow are punctuated by repeated reminders of the journey: 'Jesus travelled through towns and villages, teaching as he made his journey to Jerusalem' (Luke 13.22), and similarly 13.33–4; 17.11; 18.31; 19.11. Finally, at 19.41, after making his way through the suburbs he enters the city.

Luke, more than any other gospel writer, focuses on this destination, emphasizing that it is the location for the fulfilment of God's purposes in Jesus. Luke's account begins in the Temple at Jerusalem, when the angel appears to Zechariah (Luke 1.8–23). Jesus' temptations culminate in the Temple at Jerusalem (Luke 4.9). Jerusalem is explicitly mentioned at the transfiguration as the place where Jesus' work will be accomplished (Luke 9.11). Luke also reports resurrection appearances in the city, rather than back in Galilee (Luke 24.33–50). Consistent with all of this, Luke portrays Jesus as purposefully moving forward towards a clear goal, the holy city Jerusalem.

However, there is something of a tension here. A journey from Galilee to Jerusalem could have taken as little as a week on foot, particularly for a fit adult male who was intent on getting there. Yet in Luke's account this journey seems to take for ever. The reason he needs to insert reminders of the destination is that otherwise the reader might forget all about it. Jesus appears to be wandering all over the place, taking the scenic route at a leisurely pace. Both Matthew and Mark pass over this journey quickly. The action in their Gospels moves almost directly from Galilee to Jerusalem. Luke, however, dwells on the journey, detailing Jesus' meandering progress as he travelled to the west through Samaria, doubling back to Galilee at least once before reaching Jericho, and finally Jerusalem.

Some scholars have concluded that Luke must have been confused about the geography of Palestine, and that he sets the traditional stories about Jesus at random locations to give a flavour of historical authenticity, though without any real historical basis. But this is to introduce a false dichotomy, implying that the only options available are to wander aimlessly, or to travel quickly and in a straight line towards a destination. In Jesus' journey from Galilee to Jerusalem, we see a journey which does have a clear goal, and indeed a clear starting point, but within which the process of travelling, the period 'on the way', is also vital. Both journey and arrival are important; the outcome cannot be separated from the process. The extended, meandering journey is a powerful expression of a sophisticated theology and spirituality, not simply an indication of geographical naivety.

A number of themes can be drawn out. One important strand is the strong resonance between the journeying of Jesus and the behaviour of key Old Testament figures such as Abraham, Elijah and Moses. In Chapter 1 we noted the emphasis placed by Luke on the continuity between the kingdom of God revealed in Jesus and the heritage of ancient Israel. Both Elijah and Moses, for all their human limitations, are important models used by Luke to understand Jesus and to communicate the truth about him. In Luke's account of the transfiguration Elijah and Moses discuss Jesus' forthcoming journey with him (Luke 9.11). There do seem to be particularly close parallels between the long journey of Jesus in Luke's Gospel and the long journey of Moses and the people of Israel through the wilderness in the book of Deuteronomy. Both journeys involve challenging a rebellious and hard-hearted people, both involve the authentic teaching of God's law, in both Jericho is the entry point to the place of destiny (Deuteronomy 34.1; Luke 19.1), both involve rejection, apparent failure and death, and both are definitive for the identity and salvation of God's people. In

Luke's Gospel Jesus' mission is even described by the Greek word *exodos* (Luke 9.31). For Luke, one thing that the journey of Jesus can tell us is that he is the 'Prophet like Moses' who was promised long ago (Deuteronomy 18.15, 18), who speaks with God's authority, and who brings God's salvation (Luke 7.16; Acts 3.22; 7.27).[1]

But Luke did not just invent the journeying of Jesus for his own literary and theological purposes. The evidence from all the gospel writers is that journeying was one of Jesus' most characteristic activities, forming the backdrop to his prayer, teaching, healing and the sharing of meals. Jesus probably had some form of base in Capernaum, a conveniently central point in Galilee, but he actively embraced an itinerant ministry. He travelled from place to place proclaiming his message that 'the time has come; the kingdom of God is near' (Mark 1.15), habitually withdrawing from the crowds who pursued him, wanting him to stay longer with them, so that he could move on to some new place with his message (Mark 1.35–9; Luke 4.42).

It is easy to miss this sense of journeying. Most of us live static lives in a home, a place of work, a neighbourhood. Most teachers or religious leaders we know live in a similar way. But Jesus did not: he lived 'on the way'. And this lifestyle was not just for Jesus; he also encouraged his followers to do the same. Consider Jesus' description of his existence in response to someone who wished to follow his way: 'Foxes have holes, and birds have nests; but the Son of Man has nowhere to lay his head' (Luke 9.58). We have become so familiar with Jesus' call to his disciples to 'follow me' (for example, Luke 5.27) that we can think that this just means 'be my disciple', blind to the implication that following the travelling Jesus meant travelling oneself. His life was the model for his first followers. Thus, they too were sent out to heal the sick and to preach the kingdom, accepting hospitality where offered, but always moving on (Luke 9.1–6).

In his books about Jesus, John Dominic Crossan rightly draws attention to the radical and psychologically demanding nature of this type of ministry.[2] It gives you no conventional security whatsoever, no comfort of the familiar, no certain knowledge of where the next meal will come from, nor what the response to your message will be. There can be no confidence and authority based on being known, invited or introduced. You are constantly a stranger. Each day is like the first day at school all over again. Perhaps that is why Jesus is so often reported as reminding his followers not to be anxious or afraid.

What is it like to be on the receiving end of such a ministry? How would Jesus' journeying be experienced by someone living in a small village in Galilee? First, Jesus is accessible. He comes to you; you do not have to travel a long distance to find him. This is one significant way in which the ministry of Jesus stands in contrast to the ministry of John the Baptist. John stayed at the Jordan and people went out to him; Jesus came to them. Second, Jesus doesn't stay long. Like the kingdom he proclaims, he draws near, but he then moves on. Therefore it is vital to recognize and seize the moment. The chance may not come again. This is exactly what Zacchaeus did. One day Jesus travelled through Jericho, the people turned out to see him, and there was an encounter between Jesus and Zacchaeus. The next day, or the previous day, Jesus would not have been there. Jesus entered Jericho, he drew near, but *'he was passing through it'* (Luke 19.1).

At the beginning of his ministry Jesus, in the words of Isaiah, proclaimed 'the year of the Lord's favour', and told his audience in Nazareth that *'today* this scripture has been fulfilled in your hearing' (Luke 4.21). Jesus' travelling ministry implies that Nazareth's 'today' will soon become her yesterday, with the consequence that Nazareth needs to respond now without delay. Two of the most challenging of Jesus' responses to potential followers pick up this theme. One wishes to delay only to say farewell to his family, another to fulfil the most pious of duties – burying his father. In both cases Jesus insists that tomorrow is too late, *now* is the moment for response (Luke 9.59–62).

Luke has seen and exploited a connection between the experience of those earliest followers of Jesus and that of his readers. Luke's own term for Christian discipleship is 'the Way' (Acts 9.2; 19.23; 24.22). In drawing the historically grounded 'journeying Jesus motif' to our attention he communicates something profound about our present experience of Jesus: that it is dynamic rather than static, elusive and constantly moving on, that moments of closeness and intimacy are precious and must be savoured to the full. For Luke, even Jerusalem, that most solid rock, the scene of God's definitive act of human redemption, the scene of joyful and enlightened reunion with the resurrected Christ, the scene of the giving of the Holy Spirit, is also the place where Jesus *leaves* his disciples, continuing, as it were, on his own journey first by dying, and then by ascending.

What joy when Jesus draws near! And, as we noted in Chapter 1, how human to want to prolong or recapture the moment. There is a 'snapshot' quality to many of the gospel stories of encounter between Jesus and his followers, a sense of significant and life-changing but short-lived moments, perhaps only understood fully with hindsight. It is natural, and indeed it is one of the tasks of this book, to use those significant episodes as the basis of a more con-tinuous and enduring assurance and sense of the presence of the risen Christ. But we must never forget that Jesus cannot be cap-tured, held or controlled. He is the dynamic presence of God. This is well expressed in C. S. Lewis' description of the Christ-figure, Aslan, from the *Chronicles of Narnia*:

> He'll be coming and going . . . one day you'll see him and another you won't. He doesn't like being tied down . . . It's quite all right. He'll often drop in. Only you mustn't press him. He's wild, you know. Not like a *tame* lion.[3]

We have already observed the meandering itinerary pursued by Jesus. To the casual spectator his movements as depicted in Luke might appear to be wandering in circles. There is a sense in which this is true. And we have seen that the wandering is important. But the fact that Jesus did not take a straight line to Jerusalem should not be taken to indicate any less commitment to Jerusalem on his part.

In other areas of life we are gradually learning that process can-not easily be separated from outcome. Many today are concerned about children growing up too quickly, taking on adult concerns and responsibilities too young. Nobody saying this thinks that chil-dren should not in the end become adults: the destination is not in question. But they say that the all-important process is being rushed.

Within mathematics and the physical sciences too, we are gradually realizing that complex order and beauty can 'emerge' within non-linear, dynamic systems. Chaos theory demonstrates that it is possible for a system to be deterministic yet surprising, orderly yet unpredictable and, like the mustard seed (Mark 4.30–2), produce large-scale effects from small starting points.

> ... [T]he emergent properties of dynamic systems, especially non-linear systems, are often striking and surprising. However, there is nothing mysterious or spooky about them ... Emergent properties are a function of the mathematical specification of the system, but may not be a transparent, or even a translucent, function.[4]

These sorts of systems have been described as creative and novel, elusive and difficult to capture. Perhaps most important, where they involve directional movement, the destination is latent in the path, and emerges from it, rather than the path simply being directed at a pre-specified destination.

This is a good description of the journeying ministry of Jesus: apparently chaotic, certainly non-linear, composed of small steps, and yet in fact gathering momentum and increasing crowds (Luke 11.29; 12.1; 14.25), until a climactic fulfilment at the destination. For the observer the destination 'emerges', but for Jesus, as Luke makes clear, it emerges *from* something that has been there from the start. The final act of salvation is repeatedly anticipated along the way.

So, Jesus' wandering does have a destination. Luke also tells us that it had a purpose in the mind of Jesus, which is made very clear at the end of the account of his meeting with Zacchaeus. Jesus is seeking the lost. In Luke 14.15–24, just before the point where we pick up Luke's story, Jesus tells the story of the Great Banquet. Here, the owner of the house sends out his slave 'into the squares and the lanes of the town', 'into the roads and ditches' to bring in 'the poor, the crippled, the blind and the lame' (Luke 14.21, 23). Thus we see Jesus' apparent wandering behaviour explained. Yes, there was a straight main road to Jerusalem he could have used. However, like the slave in the story, Jesus has been sent to travel the winding, chaotic, back roads, because it is there he will find the lost who have been invited to feast in the kingdom.

At the beginning of this chapter, we noted that the context of the four parables that concern us is an ongoing journey and an ongoing argument. Here we see how the two are linked. For in his journey, Jesus was seeking people. As he passed through their towns and villages, preaching the drawing near of God's kingdom, they drew near to him, and he welcomed them. As with Zacchaeus, he enjoyed their hospitality, and together they shared food and fellowship. But herein lay the problem. For Jesus was drawing near to and sharing a meal with the 'wrong people'.

The argument

'All the tax collectors and sinners used to draw near to listen to him.' Wherever he went, this particular subsection of Jewish society gathered around him. There was something about Jesus, something about what he did and said, which attracted these people. Of course, you can't blame a preacher for who listens to him. Indeed, presumably it is a good thing if the wicked want to crowd in to hear the holy man, though one might be suspicious of their motives for being there. The problem was not with them, but with Jesus. He did not just let them hear. He welcomed them, and ate with them. Jesus took them as his friends, he relaxed with them, spent time with them, seemed to enjoy being with them. He communicated acceptance. Indeed as we have seen, the whole point of his meandering journey seemed to be to seek people such as these.

To understand the disturbance and argument that this evoked, we need to consider the wider context and world-view of these Jewish towns and villages in Jesus' day. Israel was an occupied nation under immense strain. There was an obvious struggle for day-to-day physical survival among the debt-burdened peasants, but alongside this was a struggle for the survival of the whole nation as a distinctive entity in the face of constant major cultural and spiritual threats. The identity of the Jews as God's chosen covenant people, honoured through his love with his holy presence, with the gift of a fertile land, material security and countless descendants, was being pressed by the pervasive idolatry and immorality of Greek culture and the frank aggression of Roman imperialism.

Throughout their long history the people of Israel had struggled with the issue of what being God's chosen people actually required in practice. An exclusive worshipful commitment to the Lord God and the highest standards of behaviour towards other people were fundamental (for example, the 'ten commandments', Exodus 20.1–17; Deuteronomy 5.1–12). However, generally it was thought that there was also the requirement to be distinctive and separate from the neighbouring nations and cultures (Leviticus 20.22–6; Ezra 9—10). This stood in tension with a natural tendency among many to assimilate foreign practices and beliefs. The issue of remaining distinctive was there in times of security and prosperity, but became more pressing in times of invasion, exile and occupation.

The historical books of the Hebrew Scriptures tell a story of a nation that gradually declined spiritually, morally and materially, from its heyday under King David, crucially becoming more lax in its toleration of foreign religious practices. Then came the disaster of the Babylonian invasion of Jerusalem and the Exile in 587 BC. The biblical record shows that this devastating event was interpreted as God's judgement on the nation for its ethical decadence and religious syncretism (Deuteronomy 29.10–28; 2 Kings 17.7–20; Isaiah 5.1–13; Ezekiel 39.21–4; Daniel 9).

The trauma of the Babylonian Exile led at first to deep questioning as to whether the covenant with God was still valid, of how to live a distinctive holy life in a foreign land, and how to worship God when there was no Temple. Maintaining identity as God's people remained a vitally important issue after the exiles returned from Babylon in 538 BC because the area of Palestine remained just a province of the larger surrounding empires. During the 300 years before the time of Jesus, Greek culture became highly influential in the thinking and practice of many educated Jews. Again, this was welcomed by some, and abhorred by others. But then in 169 BC a watershed event occurred whose influence was still being felt at the time of Jesus. At this time Judea was ruled by Antiochus IV of Seleucia, the powerful state to its north.

Antiochus launched an all-out attack on the Jewish religion, probably as part of a drive to weld together the whole of the Seleucid Empire into a cultural unity. This was particularly directed at border areas such as Palestine. He desecrated the Temple in Jerusalem and tried to force the people to abandon their distinctive practices and beliefs. Some were willing to comply – to betray their national identity – but not all. A rebellion led by the Maccabean family broke out, in which many great heroes, old and young, men and women, were prepared to die rather than break God's covenant. The Maccabean revolutionaries succeeded in throwing out Antiochus, rededicating the Temple, and establishing Jewish rule. It seemed that God had indeed honoured their loyalty and rescued them. But Jewish rule did not last long. Soon enough Judea was absorbed once more into neighbouring empires, and finally it came under Roman rule. The old issues returned: how to stay loyal to the covenant, how to guard one's heritage, how to maintain national identity.

So, one dominant question faced any Jewish teacher in the first century. How should Jews relate to the godless powers around them? The Pharisees had their answer. The Scriptures were clear: Israel was to be a holy nation, dedicated to God, living by his standards, separate from the impurity of the world. (By the time of Jesus the Hebrew words for 'holy' and 'separate' had come to be used essentially interchangeably.[5]) It was only when the people betrayed this calling that calamity came upon them. When they remained firm to it God had rescued them. Thus, the Pharisees spread out throughout Judea and Galilee teaching people to obey God's law in detail, encouraging them to be pure, dedicated to God alone. Frequently alongside them we find scribes, experts in the law and the sacred histories, defining for people what was right and wrong, what their God expected of them. This was a particularly strong agenda in Jesus' homeland of Galilee, for it had only become part of the Jewish nation a century or so before, under the Maccabean kings. Now was the moment for the Galileans to demonstrate their loyalty.

What of the tax collectors and sinners? There is more to these than our twenty-first-century context might suggest. Tax collectors like Zacchaeus were the agents of the Romans. They were Jews who made their living taking money from their compatriots and paying it to the hated godless powers or their puppet rulers. Like those who had sided with King Antiochus and his attempt to destroy the Jewish nation, they were seen as betraying their own calling as God's people. 'Sinners' too meant something more than people who happened to commit a sin. All Jews, Pharisees included, knew that nobody is without sin, and rejoiced that God in his mercy had provided a way of dealing with sins through the temple sacrificial system. Its rituals and practices, detailed principally in the book of Leviticus, can seem alien to us but we should not allow this to blind us to the fact there was a system for dealing with sin in the Judaism of Jesus' day. 'Sinners' does not mean everyone, but rather those who did not even try to live according to the covenant; like those whose abandonment of the covenant had six hundred years earlier led to Israel being exiled from the land. If the primary question for a religious teacher was 'How should we relate to the godless powers around us?', it strongly implied a secondary question, 'How should we deal with Jews who betray their nation and reject God?'

It is with this in mind that we need to read these verses introducing the parables. Israel was a people under immense pressure. The Pharisees, and many scribes, believed that the only hope for the nation, and with it the good of the whole people, would come from obedience to God's law and pure dedication to God alone. Thus they exhorted, encouraged and cajoled the people into a more rigorous piety. Furthermore, whether you did or didn't follow God's laws affected not just you but also your neighbours and colleagues; the first century was not as individualistic as the 'developed' West of today. The Pharisees' goal was a holy society, not just holy individuals.

It follows from this that if some Jews were betraying their calling as God's people and polluting the nation, then they should be publicly excluded. First, because of course the consequent shame and stigma would strengthen the resolve of the weak to persevere with their obedience – people could not be allowed to think that holiness is an optional extra. Second, by excluding some, the purity of the true people, however few, could be maintained. The Scriptures spoke of a remnant of the pure remaining (1 Kings 19.14–18; Zephaniah 3.11–13). In the days of the Maccabees not all Jews had joined the revolt, but God's purposes and favour had flowed through those who remained loyal.

But what of Jesus? He was a holy man, a pious Jew. He might interpret some of the laws differently from the Pharisees, but on this fundamental issue – that God requires loyalty and obedience to his covenant – what disagreement could there be? Yet his actions seemed to say the opposite. In each of the three particular stories Luke tells elsewhere of Jesus and a tax collector or sinner (Levi, 5.29–32; the woman at Simon's meal, 7.36–50; Zacchaeus, 19.1–10) others complained about the welcome and acceptance which Jesus showed them. Here in this summary the complaint is the same: 'This man welcomes sinners and eats with them!' How could he do this? He was accepting people who had rejected God and was demonstrating this acceptance publicly. In the eyes of the Pharisees he was putting himself, and thus the nation, in danger of being corrupted. What message did he think that this communicated to the poor, hard-pressed villagers who, despite their difficulties, strove to remain faithful? We need to be clear here, 'tax collectors' and 'sinners' were not 'the poor'. They were more like Jeffrey Archer than Mother Teresa. If anything, tax collectors at least were relatively well off. They were not labourers, working in the heat of the day if they could find work at all. Indeed they were making money off the back of the pious, working poor. How could this holy man proclaim acceptance of those who had rejected God?

On each of the three occasions mentioned by Luke, Jesus gives a brief response to this complaint. Here, however, in Chapters 15–16 we find an extended answer, dealing directly with this essential feature of his ministry, which created such disturbance everywhere he went. We are reminded of the context and the complaint in these opening two verses (15.1–2). We then have some sustained teaching, Jesus' defence, in four consecutive parables. The heart of this defence, to be explored in the rest of this book, is that in acting in this way Jesus is acting in accordance with God's values, indeed is demonstrating what God is like. He did not say that the tax collectors and sinners were good people. This was not an argument about whether certain actions were technically breaking the law or not. The question was not 'who are the sinners?', but 'how should we treat the sinners?' To answer this question Jesus starts to speak about how *God* treats sinners. He moves from ethical and religious teacher to theologian.

At the end of this block of teaching, in 16.10–15, we return to this context. We hear the Pharisees' response, 'They heard all that he said, but laughed at him.' They cannot accept that God is as Jesus describes; the argument is not resolved. But that is to rush ahead to Chapter 8. For now, as we begin our exploration of these parables, we simply need to note the context within which they arose – Jesus wandering and searching with an ultimate emerging purpose, challenging the core beliefs of those around him, attracting the wrong sort of people. And what was it about Jesus that attracted these social outcasts? What could possibly have been in it for them? As we shall see, they recognized that there was something about him and his message that gave rise to a hope that life could be better, that things didn't have to be this way.

Through the text of the Gospel, we can enter into this experience. Just as Jesus drew near, bringing both hope and disquiet into the villages of Galilee, as we read these parables, he can come near to us. But let us not think that we can pin him down. He draws near and then moves on, close and yet somehow strange. And are we prepared to be disturbed?

3

The heart of God

So he told them this parable: 'Which one of you, if you had a hundred sheep and lost one of them, wouldn't leave the ninety-nine in the wilderness and go after the lost one until you find it? And when you have found it, you would put it on your shoulders rejoicing. You would go home and call your friends and neighbours, and tell them, "Celebrate with me because I have found my lost sheep." I tell you that in the same way there will be more joy in heaven over one sinner who repents than over ninety-nine righteous people who do not need to repent.'

(Luke 15.3–7)

Parables

'Which of you wouldn't leave the ninety-nine sheep in the wilderness and go after the lost one until you find it?' Think about it. Think about the shepherds who would have been among the crowds in villages and farms where Jesus told this parable on his journey to Jerusalem. Which of you wouldn't leave the ninety-nine and seek for the one? They would look round puzzled. What does he mean? Is there something we are missing? Nobody would do that! The lost one is probably dead already, and who knows how long it would take to find it? Meanwhile, you stand the risk of losing far more of the other ninety-nine. And as for celebrating, if you did something this foolhardy you would hardly proclaim it to the world, and have to admit that you lost one in the first place. Does this son of a carpenter turned preacher not know anything about shepherding?

It is not just Galilean shepherds who have been puzzled by this story, as the following true contemporary incident illustrates. A

26

Sunday school teacher decided to explore the theme of 'The Good Shepherd' during a family service. He asked the children to come up to the front, to imagine that they were sheep and that they were in danger from wolves and birds of prey. But they were not to worry because he was there to take care of them and protect them, sleeping across the gate of the sheep pen. Then he asked one little boy to run and hide somewhere in the church. He set out to look for the lost child and happily brought him back to the others. 'Well, children,' he asked expectantly, 'have I been a good shepherd?' The children, who had completely got 'into role', answered unanimously, 'No! You were rotten – you forgot all about us and the wolves could have eaten us up!' Some of the little ones looked frightened. The teacher was humbled, and reflected that it might have been unwise to combine two different shepherd stories into one piece of drama.

What these children had seen is what is so often missed in the parables of Jesus. They approached the parable with untutored eyes, eyes that could see, precisely as Jesus intended it to be approached: '. . . unless you change and become like children you will never enter the kingdom of heaven' (Matthew 18.3).

This parable is not a homely illustration. That is how parables are sometimes presented to us – as illustrations, drawing on normal life to make a point, embodying an eternal truth about the universe. Whereas an academic might express the point in a clear sentence, Jesus illustrates the point with a story, drawn from everyday life, to make it intelligible to the masses. But does that description actually fit this parable? Yes, it is drawn from normal life – Jesus' parables all revolve around daily life in Galilee: day labourers, planting and reaping, families and clans. But it doesn't encapsulate a simple and easily recognizable timeless truth. Indeed, while drawing on the normal world of his hearers, it seems to contradict it. Just as Jesus in his journeying is accessible, and yet elusive, this parable seems accessible, and yet its meaning is hard to capture and to understand.

What is more, the strangeness of the parable is not hinted at in the way that it is told. Jesus doesn't say, 'I tell you a mystery . . .' or 'This a hard saying, but stick with it . . .' Instead he essentially says, 'Isn't it obvious that the world is this way?', artfully luring his hearers to respond, 'Yes – no – wait a minute!'

Part of our problem here is that we think of parables as teaching something, by which we mean something that could be distilled out and expressed in a single sentence. We think of Jesus as a modern-day preacher, who thinks of the points he or she wants to make, and then thinks of ways of illustrating them to keep the Sunday morning congregation awake. But the parables do not teach something; they challenge. They provoke us into thinking, 'Is that right? Is that how things are? Is that fair?' Earlier in this Gospel Jesus has said, 'I came to set the world on fire . . . Do you think that I have come to give peace to the earth? No, I tell you, not peace but division' (Luke 12.49–51). Jesus is troubling; he brings disturbance. We have already seen this as we considered his journeys around Galilee. In each place Jesus caused commotion. In some places, it seems to have been joy; in many, a rush to bring out the sick; often enough, arguments with the religious teachers. And then he departed, leaving the people affected, changed, pondering what had happened to them. So too with a parable. It destabilizes our notions of how things are, or how they should be. It does not so much give an answer as pose a continual question. Jesus' distinctive form of teaching – the parable – fits his distinctive itinerant mode of life.

Jesus' travels from one village to another, carrying little baggage, arriving as a stranger, presenting himself and his message on their own merits without institutional authority, made him vulnerable. It was a risky strategy. In exactly the same way, teaching in parables is risky. How tempting it is for teachers to hide behind jargon and esoteric language. This is especially true of teachers who are inexperienced or have little confidence in themselves or their message. How risky it is to use terms and models known inside out by your audience – and how dangerous to mess about with these terms. Yet this is precisely what Jesus did:

> . . . the parables tell us stories that could have happened, but it is this realism of situations, characters and plots that precisely heightens the eccentricity of the modes of behaviour to which the Kingdom of Heaven is compared.[1]

Jesus had supreme confidence in the truth he was communicating. The ease with which he can say in these parables, 'Isn't it obvious?' and then present something that is not at all obvious gives us an inkling of the authoritative impact his teaching must have had on his first audiences (Luke 4.32).

The connections between Jesus' life and teaching are particularly clear in this sequence of parables in Luke 15.1–16.17. As we saw in Chapter 2, the religious leaders were accusing Jesus of not acting like a holy man because he welcomed the wrong *people*. In response he told these stories of shepherds, women, fathers, brothers, rich men and managers. As we shall find, these stories are full of wrong *endings*. They are not like Grimms' fairy tales in which the good get rewarded, and the bad punished, where a sense of natural justice is endorsed. Such stories support the status quo, the dominant assumptions and values of society. That is why they are told to children at bedtime: 'They all lived happily ever after' is a reassuring invitation to sleep. But these parables are a wake-up call. They challenge the status quo, just as, by his behaviour, Jesus was challenging the dominant assumptions and values of his society.

The parables of Jesus are marked by incongruity ('wrong' endings), paradox (apparent contradictions), and ambiguity (more than one interpretation may suggest itself to the hearer). Paradox and incongruity are powerful ways to challenge our assumptions about ourselves and the about the way the world is. The developmental psychologist, Jean Piaget, argued that it is through the challenge to existing mental maps or 'schemas' posed by real-world incongruities that cognitive abilities advance in young children.[2] According to his theory child cognitive development is not just the continuous accumulation of knowledge about the world, but is more like a series of hypothetical models that are challenged, and then developed or replaced by new models that fit the facts better. In this respect children are rather like scientific experimenters.

It is therefore no accident that Piaget's account resonates with the model of scientific thought and practice proposed by Thomas Kuhn.[3] Kuhn repudiated the notion of continuous accumulation of knowledge in science, and instead advanced the idea of conceptual and methodological 'paradigm shifts' occasioned by experimental findings that are anomalous in terms of the current scientific status quo. The parables of Jesus are meant to instigate just such a paradigm shift in his hearers, a shift into the kingdom of God. Jesus' use of paradox in particular seems to have been unique.[4] It has not been found in the traditions of the Pharisees and rabbis of his time. This is perhaps not surprising if his agenda was to question, challenge, and thereby to transform.

Paradox has another characteristic. It can express mystery. The presence of God cannot be captured in simple propositional language or even in pictures. But the paradox of the parables is able to hold in tension the truth that God has drawn near to us, has entered the world of nature and human relationships, yet remains profoundly mysterious. For us, mystery arises when the limits of our intellectual or emotional understanding have been reached. And strangely, it is often when we are at our limits, weary, suffering, deeply confused, that we become especially aware of the presence of God (see for example Psalm 4, Psalm 31 and many others, also 1 Kings 19.10–12).

As if in confirmation of this, psychologists who study religious behaviour have observed that spiritual development seems to be associated with times of difficulty and crisis. For instance, Kenneth Pargament notes that religion and spirituality emerge in what he calls 'boundary situations', occasions in which people are confronted with the inexplicable and irresolvable limits of the world.[5] The paradoxical, incongruous, ambiguous parables of Jesus push us into such boundary situations if we let them.

But will we? Most of us do not like being challenged about how we view the world, particularly regarding religion. Fundamental beliefs are foundations that may be just too precious to be shaken. The sayings of Jesus were genuinely too hard for some (John 6.60). It is possible to dismiss them as nonsense or blasphemy as did many of Jesus' first hearers. Paradox and incongruity can often evoke laughter, as they did with the Pharisees (Luke 16.14) – a very effective way to distance oneself from the challenge they communicate. In addition, because the parables are ambiguous or open, because so much depends on what is made of them by the hearer, it is possible to draw their teeth through professional interpretation, to reduce them to simple homely truths, or to question their authenticity. If we draw the teeth from the parables, we draw the teeth from Jesus. We create a plausible Jesus who would make sense to us, who would have acted only in the ways that we think are appropriate. We can do this 'naively', expecting Jesus to act like a man living in the twenty-first-century urban West. But we can also do this 'sophisticatedly', expecting Jesus to act like our enlightened idea of a man living in first-century rural Palestine. Such a Jesus will never shock us because we have ensured he only does what we ourselves have already decided is sensible. The four parables we are studying in this book move from perplexing to disturbing to downright shocking. The final parable, the 'dishonest manager', has been the subject of more scholarly endeavour and controversy than most precisely because it is so difficult. Scholars have produced any number of detailed (and contradictory) explanations to avoid taking this parable at face value. In this they have found themselves in agreement with the Pharisees: a parable this shocking cannot be a responsible or truthful message for a religious leader to give.

These sorts of responses to the parables are, amazingly, exactly what Jesus describes in that parable of all parables, the story of the sown seed (Luke 8.5–8). Like the seed, a parable is a small and obscure thing, easily missed or dismissed, yet with the potential to open the gateway into a life that bears great fruit. Like the seed, the outcome of a parable depends entirely on its reception: it can be ignored, or it can be redefined (choked) so that the demands it makes on the hearer are not so radical. The approach of the hearer to the parable is crucial. This is why Jesus ends the story of the sown seed with, 'He who has ears to hear, let him hear.'

Jokes provide a useful parallel to parables. To work, to be funny, a joke needs to draw on human life, shared experiences and expectations, and then to introduce a twist, the unexpected, the incongruity, the 'punchline'. And its purpose is to make you laugh. Similarly Jesus' parables draw on human life, and shared experiences, and then introduce a twist, designed not so much to make us laugh as to make us think – to provoke us to reconsider

31

whether the world, whether God, is really as we have assumed. Parables need to make sufficient sense to invite engagement, but they do not need to make full sense when subjected to rigorous analysis; they do not need to be reducible to a concise logical statement recommending a particular course of action or set of beliefs. Appreciating why something is funny is not the same as laughing. In the words of the New Testament scholar, C. H. Dodd, the purpose of parables is to '... tease (the mind) into active thought'.[6] As we come now to read and ponder these parables, and through them to encounter Jesus, we must be open to this capacity to shock, to unsettle, to challenge what we think we know. In doing this we will be drawing alongside those first unsettled hearers in the villages of Galilee.

The lost sheep

'Let me tell you what God is really like.' This is what Jesus is claiming to be doing in this parable of the lost sheep – explaining to his hearers, Pharisees, sinners and others, what God is really like. This is an audacious claim. If this were a theological discussion on the nature of God, the parable might be more acceptable. But it is not. The context, as we have seen, is grumbling about Jesus' actions in welcoming the tax collectors and sinners. *Jesus'* actions are questioned, but he responds by telling this parable about how *God* behaves.

At the beginning of the parable one might not notice this. 'Which one of you would not seek for the lost sheep?' Jesus asks. His hearers would naturally think that he is telling a parable about himself, explaining why he is seeking after the tax collectors and sinners by comparing himself to a shepherd. Indeed, this is clearly what the parable is about in one sense. After all, Jesus is journeying around Galilee welcoming and, as we have seen, even searching out sinners, and so he tells a story about a shepherd searching for a lost sheep. He is presenting himself as a shepherd ignoring most of the sheep (the already religious, like the scribes and Pharisees) in order to save the lost (tax collectors and sinners). However, there is more to this, for the image of sheep and a shepherd was already well known within Judaism (Psalm 23.1; 78.52; 80.1; Isaiah 40.11; Jeremiah 31.10; Micah 7.14) finding its clearest expression in Ezekiel Chapter 34:

> My sheep were scattered over all the face of the earth, with no one to search or seek for them. Therefore . . . as I live, says the Lord God, because my sheep have become a prey, and my sheep have become food for all the wild animals, since there was no shepherd and because my shepherds have not searched for my sheep . . . thus says the Lord God, I am against the shepherds . . . I myself will search for my sheep, and will seek them out.
>
> (Ezekiel 34.7–11)

Thus, those who heard this parable and reflected on it (and presumably Jesus told it, and similar ones, on many occasions) would start to wonder if this story was explaining Jesus' actions (which is what the context would demand), or describing God's actions (which the allusion to Ezekiel might suggest). The more one thinks about this, the more disturbing this apparently homely parable becomes. What at first seems to be a defence of Jesus' actions by means of an illustration from everyday life, on deeper consideration appears to be a provocative teaching about what God is really like. This is where the brilliant ambiguity of the parables comes into its own. We have already noted that ambiguity can render a parable vulnerable to misinterpretation. But it can also enrich it, allowing two apparently incompatible interpretations to be held together, with a consequent leap forward in knowledge.

At one point in a recent public discussion between a famous agnostic writer and a Christian academic scientist, the writer asked his debating partner, 'I'm confused. Are you talking about God or Jesus here?' The scientist paused for a moment. 'Yes!' he replied. In this parable Jesus is talking about himself and he is talking about God, and the two are inseparable.

At the end of the parable the reference to God becomes explicit and its full challenge is revealed. Jesus concludes with an explanation: 'I tell you . . . there will be more joy in heaven . . .' This is a standard contemporary Jewish idiom that avoids both mentioning God's name and attributing direct action to him. It would have been understood as, 'I tell you . . . God will rejoice more . . .'

At one level this means that Jesus is claiming that God is with him, that he is acting in complete accordance with God's character. The Pharisees think that they are defending God's standards by attacking Jesus, but in fact they are opposing God because God is with Jesus. Indeed, presumably they are the shepherds who 'have not searched for my sheep'. However, the parable raises further questions. For Jesus does not explain the connection between his picture of God and his own actions. Perhaps there is no need, but there is something disturbing about someone who responds to questions about his actions with an explanation of what God is doing. And how does Jesus know what God is like? He is not merely interpreting or applying Ezekiel 34 – a bold enough step – he is adding plenty of details of his own. What Jesus is claiming, so subtly that it is easily missed, is direct, unmediated, access to the heart of God. He is saying, 'I act like God acts'; he is implying, 'I know what God is like'; and he is offering, 'If you want to know what God is like – look at me.' We are not very far from 'Whoever has seen me has seen the Father' (John 14.9).

And there is more. For Ezekiel's picture of God developed here by Jesus is also startling in itself. God is searching for the lost, like a shepherd for a sheep. This is an image that is so familiar to us that we can miss the force of it. The man in this story is the owner of a very large flock of sheep. He is, by implication, a rich and powerful man. He would have had shepherds to look after his flock for him. But he does not order his minions to find his lost sheep. He decides to look for the sheep himself. He isn't a shepherd – he chooses to *become* a shepherd. He, a rich man, chooses to take on one of the most menial and despised jobs in Jewish society. He, a powerful man, engages in an activity that by its nature throws up his human weakness and limitation (2 Corinthians 8.9; Philippians 2.7). For it is not that the sheep has gone astray, that the omniscient owner knows exactly where it is, and sets out to collect it. The sheep is *lost* and it has to be *searched* for. The image is of God himself having to work, to search out, unsure of success; enduring heat, danger, discomfort. The man seeks after his sheep 'until he has found it'. This is open-ended; it is fundamentally not under his control.

The question on the Pharisees' lips, the question that concerned John the Baptist (Luke 3.10–14), and indeed the natural question to ask is, 'What must sinners do to make things right? How can they find their way back into God's covenant people?' (rather like Little Bo Peep's sheep that, left to their own devices, must find their way home). But Jesus approaches the situation from another perspective. One of the striking things about this collection of four parables is that as they progress, the perspective on the action shifts. The first two parables are from God's point of view; in the parable of the lost son the point of view of human beings is introduced; finally, the parable of the dishonest manager is told almost exclusively from a human perspective. In this first parable Jesus introduces God's perspective.

In the process, Jesus talks about God as if he were a human being. This is nothing new. As we have seen, the Hebrew Scriptures frequently speak about God in these terms and, like Jesus, their writers would have been well aware that God is not a human being. Jesus is using metaphorical language, speaking about one thing in terms of another, talking about something that is unfamiliar in terms of the familiar. The power of metaphor lies in the richness of associations that a particular image calls up. So, when Jesus reminds us that God is like a shepherd in so far as he seeks out lost individuals, other aspects of human shepherding and seeking are called to mind. Many of these will be illuminating, some may be misleading.[7] It is important to check our exploration of this image against the text of the parable, noticing where the emphasis really lies.

In this parable Jesus is talking about God in terms of action and emotional expression – of searching behaviour and of joyful celebration. This is a highly psychological description and, if we observe our caveat of continually keeping the text in mind, human psychology can help us unpack the parable further. First it helps us to see how the parable acts on our own psychology, bringing us closer *into relationship* with God rather than merely helping us to understand more about him.

Jesus never tells us that God loves us at any point in these parables. Yet that seems an obvious conclusion. This is because we are so used to inferring the attitudes, thoughts and feelings of other people from their actions. We can guess that Zacchaeus felt loved and affirmed when Jesus called him by name and entered his home to share a meal. In the same way, as we start to identify with the lost sheep, or draw alongside the 'sinners', we apprehend that God loves us by the fact that he searches for us and communicates great joy when he finds us. Jesus is saying, 'Look at what you know about the motivation for human actions and apply it to God.' Paul does exactly this: 'But God makes his love for us clear: while we were still sinners Christ died for us' (Romans 5.8). This human ability to infer the mind-states or feelings of others from their behaviour, of putting oneself in the shoes of someone else, is called 'theory of mind'. It is strongly related to empathy, and underpins the establishment of mature, genuine, human relationships. So, when Jesus presents God to us in anthropomorphic terms he invites us to enter God's mind, to begin to empathize, to come into relationship.

Second, some insights from scientific psychology can verify and enrich the insights we have gained with our own theory of mind, can help interpret the searching behaviour of the shepherd further. In recent years neuroscientists have identified two distinct human brain-behaviour systems that underpin different sorts of searching.[8] One is characterized by curiosity, the desire to explore, to play with ideas, to experience new things. This sort of seeking is pleasurable. The second sort arises from enforced separation from a companion (human or animal). This sort of seeking is associated with distress and sadness, only removed by reunion with the lost companion. It is longing rather than predatory desire. (Contrast the search for the fox by the hunt with the search for a lost pet.) We will explore this in much greater depth in the next chapter, but first it is important to ascertain whether the searching as described in this parable corresponds to either of these human searching systems. The answer lies in the absence of any hint of pleasure or curiosity in the seeking, and in the intense joy that is expressed on reunion with the lost sheep. These are characteristic of the second sort of human searching, the sort underpinned by separation distress. Jesus does not say that God experiences separation distress (an emotion), just as he does not say that God loves us (an attitude); but both are reasonable psychological conclusions from this parable. Such ideas are also expressed elsewhere in the Bible (see for instance Hosea 11), and in Jesus' own action in weeping over Jerusalem.

However, Jesus does talk openly about God's joy. The owner turned shepherd has called his friends and neighbours, telling them 'celebrate with me'. We are not told how the sheep feels; it is the owner who is happy, so overjoyed by finding the sheep that he wants to have a party. The final sentence describes 'joy in heaven over one sinner who repents'. This is not mere satisfaction in a heavenly administrator ticking off one more box on his worksheet, glad that another job has been accomplished. There is *joy* in heaven. The longing, the searching, the endurance has borne fruit. Finding the sheep is an emotional event, and an experience to be shared with others. Celebrate with me. This mention of a celebration points us back to the accusation against Jesus of eating and drinking with the sinners (for example, Luke 7.34; 15.2): Jesus has been acting out exactly this kind of celebration.

This man's decision to go after the lost sheep is not rational, given that it could put so many other sheep at risk. It is not a decision based on a cost-benefit analysis. It is an act of the heart. He feels for the lost sheep. The losing of the sheep affects him personally. He seeks after the sheep 'until he has found it'. His actions are being driven by a longing for the sheep to be found. Yet the basis of this longing is not so much a detached consideration of the sheep's good, as it is the self-interest of the seeker. He searches for the sheep primarily to meet his own need, for 'his own name's sake' (Psalm 23.3), although it is also in the sheep's best interests. His needs and the needs of the sheep have become the same thing.

Talking about God in such emotional terms challenges many conventional ways of thinking about the divine, especially in the 'developed' West. So much in our society has taught us that emotion is something to be left behind; being serious or dispassionate is the quality one expects from those in authority. Being driven to act because of an overflow of emotion, as seems to be the case with this man, is generally seen to be a bad thing. Saying that something is an emotional reaction to a situation is often tantamount to saying it is inappropriate, to be ignored. The head should rule the heart. Lesser people might react in that way, and sometimes it is understandable, especially in a culture of postmodernity, but the ideal is to put one's emotions aside. God as creator, ruler and judge of the whole world should be no exception. He should be disinterested, dispassionate, and fair. In the history of western culture the languages of classical philosophy, the law or even science have been dominant ways of talking about God. All of these strive to 'rise above' emotion and distance themselves from the personal. Attributing emotions to God is easily dismissed as naive anthropomorphism. But Jesus describes God as a shepherd full of longing for his lost sheep, acting recklessly to try to find it, overcome with joy when he does. He is not saying here that the character of God is intrinsically emotional. He is not interested in engaging in an enterprise of systematic theology. He is commenting on, and by implication authenticating, the fact that in our *encounter* with God we, as emotional beings ourselves, may *experience him as emotional* and respond accordingly.

This parable is also about risk – the risk this man is prepared to accept in order to save the lost sheep. Indeed, as he sets out on his search he does not know whether he will find the sheep or not. He undergoes the risk for the *chance* of finding the sheep. In contrast the Pharisees were not risk-takers. They saw holiness as their aim: God is holy and so he calls his people to be holy. And holiness all too easily becomes a matter of separation from impurity; that is, it is seen negatively, as being about avoiding pollution, or avoiding sin. Such a mind-set is almost inevitably conservative: the new, the unknown, may endanger or pollute the already established. What could be gained is small compared to what could be lost. That is why the Pharisees were criticizing Jesus. His welcome of the sinners might be good for them, but in the process the holiness of the whole nation, and thus any prospects of rescue by God from their current trials, would be damaged. Their response to the situation of one lost sheep would be to build the fences higher to protect the others (a solution that might have been favoured by the Sunday school children in our anecdote). This is a response that is dominated by fear (another basic human brain-behaviour system, but one that is never attributed to God in the Bible). Yet it seems to make sense; perhaps the good of the many is more important than the possible salvation of the few? In John's Gospel we are told that this was exactly the reasoning behind Jesus' eventual execution: 'It is better for one person to die for the people than for the whole nation to be destroyed' (John 11.50). Jesus' disagreement with the Pharisees was not because they felt it was wrong to preach to the wicked, but because he seemed to be welcoming the wicked in a way that would endanger the good, chasing after the lost sheep, leaving the other ninety-nine in peril.

Nevertheless the focus of the parable is not the Pharisees but God. Of course, one would imagine that there would be implications for what the Pharisees might do, but the issues surrounding the maintenance of the integrity of the community are complicated. This parable does not give an answer. Indeed, by speaking about the shepherd, and from his perspective, and by giving pride of place to his emotions, it simply avoids engaging in the questions the Pharisees were asking. They wanted to know how Jesus' actions could possibly build up and enhance the holiness of God's chosen people. He defended his actions by challenging them to see the situation from the perspective of a God who is overwhelmed by compassion and longing for lost individuals. (For an identical argument see Luke 13.10–17.)

Let us return to Zacchaeus, for he was a chief tax collector. By definition he was a traitor to his own community, a servant of the godless in the domination of God's people. Nevertheless, Jesus described Zacchaeus as a 'son of Abraham'. Many would have thought that the tax collector had renounced or forfeited his status as one of God's chosen people by his actions. Again we see that this was not the case. He might have been 'lost' (as Jesus strongly implies by stating that he came to 'seek out and save the lost') but he was still a son of Abraham, just as in the parable the sheep still belongs to its owner even after it is lost. Indeed, he says, 'Celebrate with me because I have found *my* lost sheep.' The sheep always remained his, and however far they wandered they were still close to his heart.

Here perhaps we get to the crux of the difference between Jesus and the Pharisees. They both agreed that these people were 'sinners'. Jesus himself explicitly contrasts 'a sinner who repents' with 'ninety-nine righteous people who do not need to repent'. It is not that Jesus is saying that the sinners are not really sinners, or that they are being criticized unfairly. If we understand the parable this way, as Jesus siding with the pious poor against the self-righteous elite, we neutralize it. It is reduced to a mere difference of opinion over definitions of right and wrong. The difference here is more fundamental. Are sinners still part of God's people? If you have renounced God, have you forfeited your position? The Pharisees said yes – those who choose to reject God have to live with the consequences. Jesus claimed that God sees things differently. However much people reject him, he is still driven by compassion for them, he keeps searching for them and is overjoyed when they are found. The lone sheep in the parable is lost. The point is not that, from the enlightened perspective of its owner, the sheep is really just somewhere a little different. It is lost, and because it is lost, because it is has always been his sheep, because he cannot bear to let it go, he searches for it himself.

This parable is so familiar, and yet it is truly revolutionary. Implicitly it contains a claim about Jesus and his mission, for the way God behaves and thinks is presented as a defence of Jesus' actions. More dramatically it contains surprising teaching about the nature of God in his interaction with human beings. We hear God described in terms that suggest weakness and vulnerability, reckless risk-taking, likened to a human being who seems more emotional than cerebral in character.

Ezekiel's moving description of the lost sheep of Israel was written around the time of the Babylonian exile six hundred years before Jesus. It primarily refers to the scattering of a people who longed to go home and live united in peace and security in Jerusalem. Ezekiel's lost sheep are the Babylonian exiles and the tribes of Israel who had been lost two hundred years earlier as a result of the Assyrian invasion. But Jesus is reapplying this image to his own time, the time when God is gathering people into his kingdom, and he is *redefining what it means to be lost*. Jesus is not talking about geographical strays but about people who have got morally and spiritually lost, either through their own bad decisions, or through the socially exclusive practices of the culture they inhabit, or through a lethal combination of both.

There are times in our lives when many of us feel truly lost. Lost because we have been overcome with despair. Lost because of broken relationships. Lost because we have got stuck in negative cycles that we can do nothing to change. Lost because we have done something so bad that if people only knew what we were really like they would reject and abandon us. This parable tells us that being lost is part of the human condition, but presents to us a God who longs to find us, and who is prepared to risk everything to take us in his arms and carry us home.

4

The searching woman and the lost coin

———◦◦◦———

Or which woman, if she had ten silver coins and lost one, wouldn't light a lamp and sweep the house and search carefully until she finds it? And when she has found it, she would call her friends and neighbours* saying, 'Celebrate with me because I have found the silver coin which I had lost.' In the same way, I tell you, there is joy in the presence of God's angels over one sinner who repents.

(Luke 15.8–10)

(* The Greek makes clear that these are female friends and neighbours.)

'Or,' says Jesus, 'to put it another way. . . .' This second parable in our sequence of four is very similar to the first. The structure is the same and many of the same phrases appear in both ('until she has found it', 'when she has found it', 'call her friends and neighbours', 'celebrate with me because I have found . . .', 'in the same way there is joy', 'over one sinner who repents'). It is easy to see it as a postscript to the previous parable; certainly commentators often pass over it briefly, seeing it merely as a different illustration of the same point. But this is to miss so much. For, as we have seen, a parable is not merely an illustration, a way of clothing a basic point. Of course it is true that this parable is similar to the previous one. But it is a distinct story, with different characters, and it challenges in different ways, bringing new points into focus. The second parable does not merely restate the message of the first in an alternative guise – it complements it, develops it, and clarifies it. It is, if anything, more disturbing. For while the setting and activity described would have been comfortably familiar to the first hearers, the choice of protagonists is radical: a woman rather than a man and a coin rather than a sheep.

The searching woman

One of the distinctive aspects of Luke's writings is what has been described as 'gender complementarity' – the tendency to balance males and females. There are numerous examples in Luke's Gospel. These include Zechariah and Mary (Luke 1), Simeon and Anna (2.25–38), the widow of Nain's son and Jairus' daughter (7.11–17; 11.40–56) and, as we noted in the previous chapter, the woman with the curved spine and Zacchaeus – a lost daughter and a son of Abraham (13.10–17; 19.1–10). The man searching for his sheep and the woman searching for her coin is one of these 'gender pairs'.

In emphasizing the pairing of male and female in this way Luke is drawing out something that is also there in more subtle guise in Matthew's Gospel. This tells us that while Luke was particularly aware of 'gender pairs' in the teaching of Jesus, they are not unique to his writings. In Matthew 6.25–30 we find the birds of the air (male occupation of sowing and reaping) and the lilies of the field (female occupation of spinning). Matthew and Luke share men working in the field/lying in bed and women grinding corn (Matthew 24.40, 41; Luke 17.34, 35) and the pairing of the man sowing the seed and the woman mixing yeast into flour (Matthew 13.31–3; Luke 13.18–21). Jesus' teaching using pairings of this sort emphasizes that the kingdom of God includes male and female in harmonious balance. At a very practical level it shows that he drew close to people, making himself and his message accessible in terms of their gender identity. There is no sense in which the kingdom is described as centred on males, with females in a subsidiary or spectator role.

The parables of the lost sheep and the lost coin balance a male activity in a pastoral setting with a female activity in a domestic setting. This has caused concern to some feminist commentators, who note the restricted domain of most women at the time of Jesus. Whereas men moved freely between the home and the outside world, respectable women stayed at home ('her indoors'). In these parables both the man and the woman are searching to the furthest extent of their worlds, and the woman's world is small.

43

But Jesus is here primarily connecting with 'where people are now', not putting them into an idealized situation of where they ought to be. He is raising up and honouring the apparently humdrum everyday activities of women and men in the real time and place of first-century Galilee by saying, 'What you are doing is like the activity of God.'

How would those first women who heard this parable have received it? An interesting study that sheds some light on this was carried out by Carol Schersten LaHurd in the early 1990s.[1] She interviewed Arab Christian women from Egypt and the Lebanon about their reaction to the story, and she also observed the lives of Arab Muslim women in North Yemen, who inhabit a social world that is in many ways similar to that of first-century Palestine. From this she drew the following observations. First, the women responded to the accuracy of the domestic detail in the parable – the need to light a lamp in order to search properly in a house with few and small windows, the need to use a broom, perhaps a date palm branch, to make sure every square inch had been covered. Secondly, the female protagonist was understood to have a powerful role in the domestic arena, which is the centre from which the Arab family goes out into the wider world and to which it returns. She was assumed to be the keeper of the family purse – perhaps not a very big purse, as the silver coin involved would be a day's wages for a manual labourer – but the totality of the family's possessions all the same.

This Arabic understanding of the centrality of the home, the raising of its status in relation to the public arena, counters the cultural assumption of the industrialized twenty-first century that the home is a second-class environment. The home was a place where a woman moved freely, where she could invite her female friends and family, and where she could wield significant if subtle power. The picture that is painted in this parable of the first-century equivalent of a 'girls' night in', an autonomously thrown party to celebrate the finding of the coin, is moving, authentic, and has its counterpart in many societies.

Jesus enjoyed eating with people, and he enjoyed eating with them *at home*. The first thing he did when he encountered

Zacchaeus was to invite himself to his home. Perhaps Zacchaeus was married. Perhaps Mrs Zacchaeus was a conventional lady, or a shunned lady, who did not often leave the house. If so, on this occasion there was no need for her to do so. Jesus came into her home. This coming into homes is another key pattern of the ministry of Jesus and his disciples, seen clearly in his instructions on sending out the twelve (Luke 9.4) and the seventy-two (Luke 10.5–7). It is a pattern that continued with the first churches. Churches were meetings in people's homes. Some households mentioned in Luke and Acts were actually headed by women such as Martha, Mary the mother of John Mark, Lydia, and Chloe. Even where a man was clearly the 'head' of the family, the home was in most senses the domain of the woman. In this setting women had access to the gospel to a degree that just could not have been possible in more public spaces such as the Temple or market place. Indeed, some scholars trace a movement within Luke-Acts from a focus on the Temple to a focus on the home. At the very beginning of Luke's Gospel these two locations occur alongside each other as part of a gender pair, an angel appearing to Zechariah in the Temple and to Mary in her home. Some interesting observations about the relationship between Temple and house in Acts are made by Turid Karlsen Seim:

> Those who believe in Jesus continue to fulfil the demands of the Law concerning the temple, but their worship is not bound to particular times and places. It is emphasised that both men and women take part together in private gatherings; here they do not need to follow the temple's gender-segregated organisation, which permitted women to enter only the women's forecourt. It is also noteworthy that the Holy Spirit comes over them like a rushing wind in the house where they are all gathered – and not in the temple . . . both men and women are filled with the Spirit . . .[2]

None of this is to assert that at the time of Jesus, or in the culture in which the early Church emerged, women enjoyed the freedoms from social restrictions and sexist attitudes that we would wish for our daughters today. It is instead to caution against distorted and anachronistic readings of the New Testament texts to conform to a message either of the liberation of women or the oppression of women, when these were not part of their agenda.

Jesus' teaching affirms that women and men enjoy equal access to God's kingdom. What is more, the traditional work activities of women and men, the social and physical domains in which they move, can express the activity and nature of their Creator and Redeemer. It is interesting to explore the 'woman as banker' idea further. The woman in the parable of the lost coin is depicted as an active and responsible keeper of resources. These resources would have supported her family or perhaps her business. In Acts Luke presents some examples of eastern Mediterranean business-women (Tabitha in Acts 9.39; Lydia in Acts 16.14,), who had extended essentially domestic activities such as weaving into commercial ventures. Luke tells us that Jesus and the male disciples were supported by a number of women 'out of their own resources' (Luke 8.3).

Thus the skilled domestic and commercial activities – the *work* – of women are to be highly valued. Women are not depicted as aesthetic objects, erotic objects (note Jesus' damning repudiation of this attitude to women in Matthew 5.28) or reproductive machines in the teaching of Jesus, but as *workers*. This is true even of Mary and Martha (10.28–42), where the contentious issues are the nature of the work and the attitude taken (distracted domestic work versus focused undertaking of instruction), not the fact that both women are working. The work of women tells us about the work of God. God's kingdom spreads like the yeast that a woman mixes into flour. When a woman loses a coin and single-mindedly searches for it, for the moment forgetting everything else, throwing a hen party in her joy when it is found, we see a picture of the single-minded search of God for the people that he (or she) has lost.

This depiction of the divine in female terms would have been shocking to many of Jesus' hearers, just as it is to some today. There was, of course, a tradition of using feminine metaphors for God within the Hebrew Scriptures. For example, in the book of Isaiah, God is compared to a mother in the drama and power of childbirth, in her love for her children, in her comfort for them (Isaiah 42.14; 49.15–18; 66.13). In Proverbs Chapter 8 and in the Jewish wisdom literature that developed from it (such as Sirach 24.1–8 and the Wisdom of Solomon 7.21–9.4), God's own wisdom is personified as a woman. Nevertheless, as far as we can ascertain, these ideas were not of particular importance in the Judaism of Jesus' day, for these feminine metaphors are rarely used in Jewish writings of that time. Furthermore, these particular female images may not necessarily have done much to dignify real Jewish women. God's wisdom is not personified as a normal woman, but as an aristocratic, ethereal figure with whom few would identify. Alongside all this, we need to recognize the strong cultural assertion of the superiority of men. We see this in the wider Greek world exemplified by the work of the hugely influential Greek philosopher Aristotle (for example, *Politics* 1254b2–10: 'Again, the male is by nature superior, and the female inferior; and the one rules, and the other is ruled') reflected in Jewish writers of Jesus' day (for example, Josephus, *Against Apion* 2.200, 'The law says that a woman is worse than a man in all things'). Note how Josephus explicitly relates this attack on women to the law – for him at least it is an integral part of Jewish teaching. Finally, a standard daily prayer in the synagogue included giving thanks to God because he 'did not make me a woman'.[3] Of course beliefs on this issue, as on any other, will have varied; yet the general tone of the culture is clear.

Like the story of the lost sheep, the story of the lost coin has something of a 'wrong ending' with a celebration that is perhaps over the top. The real incongruity, however, is provided by the wrong hero: he is a heroine. Furthermore, she is not some idealistic figure of a woman, but a real woman, just like the village women standing in the crowd. The story of the Good Samaritan provides a partial parallel here (Luke 10.25–37). In this story the wrong ending and wrong hero are combined: the moral example is provided by a despised Samaritan. However, while the story of the Good Samaritan can be read as a simple story of human ethics (though of course there is more to it), the story of the lost coin is clearly about Jesus and about God. So Jesus is going beyond an inclusive attitude to women and in some sense communicating to his hearers that God is like a woman. But this is not the 'punch-line'. The story does not tell of a person searching and then reveal to the surprise of the audience that this person is a woman. Jesus begins with the *assumption* that to talk about God in female terms is quite natural. Here again we have the 'isn't it obvious?' scenario. Jesus is not saying, as he does in the great banquet, 'A man threw a party and invited some surprising people.' He is not saying, 'Women are invited to the party too.' He is saying, 'A *woman* threw a party.' The implications of this may have been shocking to some of Jesus' first hearers. But he appears to have been completely at ease with the idea, just as he seems to have been completely at ease in the company of real women (John 4.27).

In each of the parables of the lost sheep, the lost coin and the lost son, God is represented as a different human being. But what strange human beings! A wealthy man who gets his hands dirty as a shepherd chasing after his sheep, a female financial manager, a tender-hearted 'new man' of a father. And again our response is, 'Yes – no – wait a minute!' Why not a male manager? Why not a mother for the prodigal son? Surely the most telling illustration of God's searching for his people is that of a mother who has lost her child, desperate in her anguish, having been cut off from someone who was once part of her own body. Why doesn't Luke's Gospel tell us about a *woman* searching for her lost son?

But of course it does. The woman is Mary. And she has lost Jesus.

One rather strange feature of the Gospel of Luke is the ambivalent attitude to motherhood that runs like a thread through the text. Much of the first two chapters are devoted to the stories of Elizabeth and Mary, both honoured through miraculous conceptions and destined to bear special sons. The account of the birth and childhood of Jesus is told from Mary's point of view, and Mary, not Joseph, is dominant in the action. Mary prophesies at length in the words of the Magnificat, and describes herself as 'the servant of the Lord' (Luke 1.48), the only person in the New Testament who is spoken of in these highly charged terms from Isaiah. Mary co-operates with God in the mystery of the incarnation.

In all these ways the role of mother is presented as special, holy and exalted. Yet it is also made very clear that any honour and respect due to Mary are not primarily on account of her motherhood, but because her co-operation in the bringing of Jesus into the world was an act of obedience to the word of God (Luke 1.38; 8.21; 11.49). And alongside this, and at a number of points throughout the Gospel, attention is drawn to a dark side to motherhood.

The first inkling of this is Mary's wrapping of Jesus in cloth and laying him in the feeding trough[4] after his birth (Luke 2.7), which foreshadows the wrapping of the body of Jesus in burial cloth and his laying in a tomb by Joseph of Arimathea (Luke 23.53). The anticipation of the loss of her son is flagged up more clearly by Simeon, who tells her that the fulfilment of Jesus' destiny, in particular his rejection, will involve deep sorrow passing right through her soul (Luke 2.35).

The narrative moves quickly on to an episode that might be entitled 'The lost son'. In an account full of authentic psychological detail, Luke tells of the separation of Mary and Joseph from the 12-year-old Jesus. Jesus is entering adulthood. In our culture this is the age of adolescence, often marked by the loss of the unconditional love, emotional closeness and physical companionship of the earlier parent-child relationship. It is a time when parents have to begin to accept the permanent loss of the affectionate babies and toddlers they once knew, and the emergence of surly, withdrawn or confrontational teenagers. Teenagers go out alone. They come back late or stay overnight with unspecified friends. Sometimes they do not come back at all. Teenagers and young adults can make themselves emotionally unavailable. This is part of the sadness of parenthood. The inevitable 'goodbye' is there from the beginning, expressed as a series of goodbyes at school gates, airports, weddings and, more exceptionally as in the case of Mary, on the occasion of the death of a child. The desperate love of parents for their children renders them vulnerable to unparalleled anxiety at the prospect of their loss, and to unparalleled anguish if this loss is realized. This is implicitly acknowledged in

Jesus' words to the 'daughters of Jerusalem' on his way to cruci-fixion (Luke 23.28–9); in times of tribulation it is better to be childless.

Mary and Joseph search for Jesus for three days (just as the dis-ciples lose Jesus for three days after the crucifixion). When they find him his mother adopts a completely authentic accusatory tone, treating her son more like a child than like the adult he is becoming. She is relieved and angry at the same time because Jesus has caused her 'anxiety' (the Greek at this point indicates deep pain, distress and worry). She is describing separation distress.

In the previous chapter we discussed the searching behaviour that accompanies separation. This is a form of 'attachment behav-iour' technically known as 'proximity seeking', first systematically described by the anthropologist Mary Ainsworth, and it can be seen most commonly in young children who have become separ-ated from their parents.[5] But it is also seen in adults under condi-tions of stress and danger. As we write, this phenomenon is being played out in dramatic and poignant form in the aftermath of the Asian tsunami.

Early psychological research on attachment and separation concentrated on the feelings of young children. In recent years attention has turned to the feelings of parents, especially mothers. In general, parents do not need their small children in order to feel safe, so the relationship between child and parent is not strictly symmetrical. Nevertheless most mothers do seem to have a strong, biologically based need to care for their children,[6] and this involves maintaining proximity with them. In addition, the boundary between the small child and the mother's body is rather blurred because of the process of gestation, birth and breast-feeding (alluded to in some detail at various points in Luke's Gospel). For a mother, therefore, the experience of losing a child can be some-thing like a physical amputation.

In attaching himself to the Temple Jesus is asserting an identity that does not depend on his earthly parents, setting his heavenly Father in direct opposition to Joseph (Luke 2.48–9). This is the central point of the narrative. But its implications for his earthly parents, especially Mary, are also significant. They find him and, like the lost sheep, he is taken home. He is restored to his parents 'in body', but not entirely 'in spirit', and we are told that Mary continues to hold this highly charged separation experience in her heart. Much later she will lose Jesus to his destiny on the cross.

There is real sensitivity and empathy for the anguish of maternal loss in Luke's Gospel. We are told that when Jesus encounters the widow of Nain, who had just lost her son, he is overcome with compassion (literally 'gutted') for her, and both Matthew and Luke recount that when Jesus himself weeps at his rejection by Jerusalem he compares himself to a mother hen (Matthew 23.37; Luke 14.34). When Luke recounts Jesus' reflections on humanity's repeated rejection of God (Luke 11.45–52) he includes a reference to God's wisdom that makes use of the strand within Judaism which describes the divine in feminine terms. (Luke 11.49: 'Therefore the Wisdom of God said, "I will send them prophets and apostles, some of whom they will kill and persecute."')

In exploring the feelings of mothers who have lost their children, and in particular Mary, Luke's Gospel enriches our understanding of a God who has lost his people, and who sets out to find and restore them. In linking female figures such as the mother hen and the wisdom of God, with feelings of rejection, Jesus is demonstrating that the quintessential image for the feeling of God for his lost people is feminine. In the parable of the lost son, which we shall consider in the next chapter, this is balanced by a focus on a father. This father, like many men, remains silent about his feelings of loss or rejection. Not so Mary, not so the widow of Nain, and not so Jesus. In his empathy with suffering women and his use of female imagery Jesus is giving permission for us to think of God not only as strong and loving, but as vulnerable and hurting. Women can be strong (like Deborah). Men can be vulnerable (like Hosea). God is neither male nor female, but perhaps the closest we can get to understanding the yearning nature of his hurt is to consider a mother who has lost her child:

> . . . is not the sorrow of Mary the human reflection of, and the beginning of, a Christian participation in the grief of the divine Father over the death of his Son?[7]

The blameless coin

'Who is to blame?' is a recurring question in our society. We find it hard to believe that accidents happen, or that dedicated, honest people make what in hindsight can be seen as mistakes. There are good reasons for this, and they relate to our assumption that the world is a meaningful place. Most of us believe at some level that the nature of our relationship with the world is neither random not unpredictable. Where this belief is threatened by events, we respond by trying to 'make sense' of what has happened. The piles of flowers that are now routinely left at the scene of tragic accidents or crimes are often accompanied by cards on which the single word 'Why?' has been written.

Even when we understand intellectually that misfortune occurs at random, at a deeper level we tend to work with the assumption that there is a relationship between a person and what happens to him or her. Thus 'Why?' questions develop into 'Why me/him?' questions. We have a rough and ready 'theory of events' that tends to be arranged around the concepts of control and justice. Bad things may happen to people because of habitual bad choices (control) or because of some moral failing (justice). Thus 'Why?' questions develop into 'What have I/has he done to deserve this?' questions. This belief in 'person-outcome contingency' is reassuring because it implies that if we are sufficiently careful and/or sufficiently good, bad things cannot touch us.[8]

Locating causes within the person rather than in the total situation is the essential component in blaming. 'Blaming' others for their misfortunes is comforting. It distances us from threat. It asserts the predictability and controllability of the world. For instance if a friend who smokes and is overweight has a heart attack we will be concerned for her, but we may also feel slightly smug. If a friend who has a healthy diet and lifestyle has a heart attack we may start to be concerned for ourselves. Even blaming ourselves can be comforting because it gives us options for change. If I believe that my heart attack was caused by my smoking I can reappraise it as a 'warning signal', change my behaviour, and establish hope. If I believe it was a random statistical event then there is nothing I can do to avert another attack, and I may despair.[9]

The book of Job deals with this issue with great courage and at some length. Job's comforters are convinced that he must have done something to have brought about his misfortunes. Job's problem is that he is convinced that he has not, and he struggles with alternative explanations including the hypothesis that God is unjust or even malicious (Job 11—14). In the New Testament perhaps the clearest expression of the attempt to assign blame for misfortune comes in John 9.2: 'His disciples asked him, "Rabbi, who sinned, this man or his parents, that he was born blind?"'

So, the 'blame game' is not new. Jesus and the Pharisees agreed that 'the sinners' were lost, but they seemed to disagree on the issue of blame. For the Pharisees the issue was straightforward: the sinners and tax collectors only had themselves to blame. They had, by their own choice, abandoned the covenant and their nation. Of course there may have been 'hard luck stories' behind some of them, but there are always excuses, and for every person who reacted to a bad situation by abandoning loyalty to the covenant and the people, there was always another who bore the same pressures without succumbing. The key question was 'what does God require of sinners?', and the answer was, like the person who smokes and has had a 'warning' heart attack, for them to admit their culpability, repent and change their ways.

The parable of the lost coin clashes with this perspective. For what can you require from a coin? In the parable of the sheep, you could at least try to suggest that the sheep wandered off; that it was responsible for the fact that it was lost. Indeed, in Matthew's Gospel the same parable is recounted in the context of discussing relationships within the Christian community, and the lost sheep is explicitly said to have 'wandered off' (Matthew 18.12–14). But how can this be applied to a coin? The coin cannot be blamed for being lost. If anyone is to blame, presumably it is the woman.

Thus the parable of the lost coin forces us to engage with the issue of culpability. This was implicit in the parable of the sheep. For while one can try to *blame* a sheep for wandering off, on reflection this is rather strange – to what extent has the sheep done it deliberately? (though we are surprisingly adept at ignoring the strange implications of our existing beliefs). With the coin no such option is left open. The situation is stripped down to its bare essentials, and they do not include the issue of blame. The focus is purely on the woman, on God. Jesus is challenging his hearers to accept that what is really at the heart of the situation is the simple fact that these people are lost, and that God is seeking to save/find them. The reason that they *became* lost is of little consequence; what is important is the fact that they *are* lost.

Jesus even makes use of a medical metaphor. He describes lost people as 'sick', says nothing about how they became sick, nothing about advisable dietary or lifestyle changes on their part, but simply describes himself as the 'doctor' (Luke 5.31).

It is as if God is saying to a classroom of arguing children, 'I don't care who started it!' This is an extraordinarily difficult message to hear because it feels so unfair, especially when you know very well who started it, and we shall explore this sense of injustice in much more depth in Chapter 7. For now we should note that this parable invites us to reflect that a situation, which to humans is full of guilt, blame and responsibility, is to God a loss or separation. A situation of human seeking after enlightenment or purification (like that of Zacchaeus) is, to God, his own searching. A situation that involves human turning or repentance is, to God, a finding or reuniting. The inanimate nature of the coin, its very passivity, forces us to take God's viewpoint. This parable may be surprising in its challenge to the human tendency to assign blame and to require reparative action as a condition of a restored relationship, but it does match the experiences of those who describe their first encounter with Christ as being 'found' or even 'chased' by him.[10] They had not consciously been seeking God, they had not even considered themselves 'lost'. Nevertheless God found them, just as the woman did the coin.

In the same way, the lost coin sharpens the issue raised in the parable of the lost sheep, of who benefits from the finding. In the case of the sheep one could argue that, although the parable focuses on the shepherd's joy, it is greatly to the sheep's benefit to be found. But the lost *coin* does not benefit from being found: it would make no difference to the coin if it were still lost in the corner of the room. The finding benefits the woman. It is God, not the sinner, who throws a party for her friends. We are reminded once again of the experience of parents searching for their lost child. All too often the child has not been perturbed by 'being lost', if indeed he or she was aware of it at all. The anxiety and therefore the joy of finding lies exclusively with the parents. God is more pleased when we are saved, than we are ourselves. Of course human beings benefit from salvation, but these parables remind us that the joy of salvation is the joy of God.

As we discussed at the beginning of this chapter, all four parables – the lost sheep, the lost coin, the lost son, and the dishonest manager – need to be taken together. They illuminate the same situation from different perspectives. The mention of repentance at the end of the story of the lost coin reminds us of this. For repentance is not a realistic activity for a coin: it links to the previous parable, and to the overall context of Jesus' meeting with sinners. In any meeting between God and real human beings there is both divine action and human response. Indeed, as we have seen, the very genre of parable itself emphasizes this need for human response, since parables provoke their hearers to thought. This response is given full weight in the next parable, which depicts the human encounter with God very differently, in terms of human activity and divine passivity. The lost son comes to his senses and returns home. The father is waiting for him, not searching, just waiting. But that is to rush on to more familiar, though not necessarily more comfortable, territory. The parable of the lost coin is disturbing because it depicts God's response to the lost as a woman searching for a coin. God's eternal longing for his people has resulted in his saving action in Jesus' seeking and coming close to the lost in a specific time and place. And, as the lost are found and come close to Jesus, God experiences infinite joy. It is all about God.

5

The lost son

———◆◆◆———

He said: 'There was a man with two sons. Now the younger one said to his father, "Father, give me the share of your possessions which I will inherit". So he divided his property between them. A few days later, the younger son assembled all that he had and left for a distant country and squandered his possessions in wild living. When he had spent everything, a severe famine struck the whole country and he became desperately in need. So he went and attached himself to a citizen of that country who sent him into the fields to look after his pigs. He would have been happy to fill himself with the pods that the pigs were eating, but nobody gave him anything. When he came to his senses he said, "How many of my father's hired workers have bread to spare, and yet I am here dying of hunger. I will get up and go to my father and say, 'Father, I have sinned against heaven and in your sight; I am no longer worthy to be called your son. Treat me like one of your hired workers.'" And so he got up and went to his father.'

(*Luke 15.11–20a*)

The story of the lost son falls naturally into three parts. The first focuses on the lost son, the second on the meeting between the lost son and his father, and the third on the older brother. We will examine each of these in turn in Chapters 5, 6 and 7. The central section, which describes the joy of the father as he is reunited with his son, almost exactly parallels the stories of the lost sheep and the lost coin. This meeting also forms the heart or pivot of the whole block of teaching beginning at Luke 15.1 and ending at Luke 16.17. The central verse is 15.24: '"for this son of mine was dead and is alive again: he was lost and has been found!" And they began to celebrate.'

This encounter of son and father is sandwiched between accounts of the actions, motivations and feelings of the two sons. It is as if this story, in many ways very similar to the two parables that have gone before, is told to address some of the 'Yes – but . . .' questions that arise from them. It takes the human perspective seriously. This development of the basic point – that in Jesus God is seeking and saving the lost – results in an extended and beautifully symmetrical narrative with some detailed characterizations.

It is natural to ask about the identities of the characters and about what or whom they represent. Is the story about Jesus enjoying the company of the wrong people, or about God welcoming outcasts home into his kingdom, or is it about the experience of the individual believer throughout history as she or he encounters God? The answer is almost certainly '*All of the above.*'

In Chapter 3 we noted that the ambiguous nature of the parables enables Jesus to talk about himself and God interchangeably, to slip in almost unnoticed the assumption that Jesus' relationships with individuals and God's relationship with his people are one and the same. So, the lost son represents both the particular sinners who were welcomed by Jesus and all the lost people whom God wants to welcome.

There is something about the life and teaching of Jesus that individuates our relationship with God. God acted for the many through the life and death of the individual man, Jesus, as Paul asserts clearly in Romans 5.15. Corporate questions about the people of God are raised by Jesus' behaviour in relation to individuals, and he answers such corporate questions in terms of the stories of individuals. In some ways this is natural and unremarkable. The individual can be understood as the corporate in microcosm. But it also emphasizes God's concern for individuals for their own sakes: one simple conclusion that can be drawn from the story of the lost sheep is that the single individual matters as much as the ninety-nine. It is therefore not surprising that later generations have found the stories of Jesus – above all the story of the lost son – to speak so powerfully to the concerns of individuals.

So, the story of the lost son refers both to the coming in of God's lost people at the right time, and it refers to the resumption of a relationship with God at the right time in the lives of lost individuals like Zacchaeus. It was compelling then and remains compelling now precisely because it is a psychological story about the relationship between three particular people. As we consider this story further we will see that it is deeply theological in character. It develops the 'seeking' theology of the previous two parables, exploring the nature of human sin, together with divine justice and salvation, not through propositional argument, but through a narrative about our experience of encounter with God.

In this chapter we shall consider the lost son. We are told quite a lot about his thoughts and motives, and it is through these that the human perspective is finally introduced into this block of teaching, which up till now has been essentially concerned with the divine. We will examine the young man's behaviour in some depth using appropriate insights from contemporary psychology. We can do this because it is a person, not an animal or an object, that has got lost. In the previous chapter we pointed out that it made very little sense to blame a sheep or a coin for getting lost. With the intro-duction of a human protagonist the issues of moral responsibility and blame are dealt with head-on.

Prostitutes and pigs

The story begins with the son asking for a 100 per cent advance on his inheritance. At first glance this seems to represent nothing more than the gross impetuosity and impatience of youth. Why wait until you are too old to enjoy your money? 'Live now, pay later', rather than prudent saving for old age. Consistent with this, the father doesn't appear to be that bothered. We are told that he simply divides his property between his two sons.

But there is far more to this situation than meets the eye. In the context of first-century Jewish culture the son is violating all sorts of norms. First, he is demanding what would in the course of time be due to him as just recompense for working in the family business and caring for his parents in their old age. Yet he is intending neither to work for his father, nor to care for him. Second, by taking his inheritance he is presumably making his father poorer, depriving him (and the rest of the family) of the income from half of the estate. Third, and most significantly, he is effectively saying, 'Hurry up and die!' or 'I wish you were already dead!' Thus, in effect, he is renouncing any loyalty to his family; breaking it up for his own benefit. Careful research carried out among Arab Christian pastors from across the Middle East in the second half of the twentieth century by Kenneth Bailey[1] has confirmed that this sort of behaviour would have been seen as utterly reprehensible. Not only that, it is extremely unlikely that any father in this culture would agree to his son's request. We are again faced with the incongruity we have already seen in the earlier parables. If those first listeners had tried to guess what words would follow the son's request they would most likely have said, 'So he beat his son and cast him out without a penny!' not, 'So he divided his property between them.'

This surprise alerts the listener, makes us wonder what the outcome will be, whether the young man will get his just deserts, whether the father is weak or mad or both. In Chapter 6 we will pursue these questions further. At present we are concerned with the behaviour of the son.

The young man travels to a distant land; he separates himself from his father as far as possible. There is no hope of the first-century equivalent of his dropping in for an evening or coming home for the weekend. He is out of contact, effectively on the other side of the world; happy it seems to ignore the family that he has already done so much to reject. He then spends all his money. He doesn't use it to set himself up in a respectable business. He certainly doesn't send any income home. He squanders his birthright, like Esau (Genesis 25.31), seeing it only as a means to meet his immediate needs, not as a privilege to be cherished.

But it is the way that the young man spends his money that is most important. He is said to have enjoyed wild living, and later in the story it is spelt out that much of the money has been spent on prostitutes. In modern English, prostitution can have both a literal meaning referring to commercial sex, but also a pejorative metaphorical meaning referring to 'selling out', compromising high principles to gain material or social advantage. At the time of

Jesus the notion of prostitution was also metaphorically rich, but in additional ways.

In the Old Testament, prostitution and adultery are widely used as images both of Israel's unfaithfulness to God and of her moral bankruptcy (see for instance Isaiah 1; Ezekiel 16; Hosea 9). In occupied first-century Palestine prostitution flourished for simple commercial reasons. The occupying forces had sexual desires that were met by local women. For women without family or other protection this was one way, perhaps the only way, to make a living. In Matthew's Gospel (Matthew 21.31, 32) prostitution and tax collection are lumped together, presumably because they represent the two worst types of sin or, more accurately, two expressions of the same sin (another gender pair!). It is perhaps significant that this reference occurs in the context of the story of the two sons, which many scholars see as a truncated version of the story of the prodigal son in Luke.

What did prostitution and tax collection have in common? First, in the context of first-century Palestine, they both involved doing business with, and in a sense supporting, the Roman occupation. Second, and more fundamentally, they involved pollution. In both of these occupations money changed hands, and both were associated with orifices and bodily emissions. This is obviously literally true of prostitution, but we shall argue that in a symbolic sense it is also true of tax collection. The money handled by the tax collectors was tainted because, as we discussed in Chapter 2, it was essentially extorted from honest Jews, paid to the Romans, and used to line the pockets of its collectors. It was 'dirty money'. Sigmund Freud has done much to draw our attention to the fact that money and faeces are strongly associated in many human cultures.[2] Expressions such as 'filthy-rich' and 'Where there's muck there's brass' are indicative of this and communicate the sense that tax collectors like Zacchaeus were not just seen as engaging in wrong actions, but as soiled. Both the prostitutes and tax collectors were betraying the nation: their actions brought shame and pollution into the 'body politic'. Women who have sexual relations with members of occupying forces are seen as bringing shame upon an occupied nation ('they are taking our women'). Men who benefit financially from occupying forces are seen in a similar light ('they are taking our money'). The worst of it is that 'they' are not only taking it; we, our own people, are giving it to them.

In her groundbreaking book *Purity and Danger*, Mary Douglas presents an account of pollution beliefs and their associated rituals in human societies.[3] Such beliefs appear to fulfil a range of psychological and social functions, but perhaps the most important, especially in minority groups, is to support notions of tribal or national identity and stability. Put simply, if the culture can be kept hygienic by certain rituals it can be rendered safe from disorder and chaos. If there is a place to put dirt there is order and structure – 'A place for everything and everything in its place'. This need for reassurance, for order and structure, is at its greatest when the identity and survival of the culture are threatened, when ritual can move from being a means of maintaining the status quo to being an act of defence against an external source of danger. This renders the mind-set of the Pharisees more intelligible. As we saw in Chapter 2, they saw the threat to God's covenant people on all sides. So they extended and intensified the requirements of the law, safeguarding it and the people, by 'erecting a fence' around it, and making it possible for individuals to achieve a sense of order in their lives.

Douglas also argues that pollution beliefs are not arbitrary, but have specific symbolic significance. She points out that the human body can be seen as a microcosm of the nation. Bodily orifices are essentially gates in the boundary of the body, and therefore signify breaks in the boundaries of the nation. Thus, at the level of the body, people who are losing or exchanging vital fluids through orifices are living at the margins, blurring the boundaries of what is in and what is out. At the level of society, people who associate intimately with other cultures are also living at the margins. Both sorts of marginal people, in their different ways, are polluters, and prostitutes are polluters at both levels. They threaten national purity, and would have been avoided by most respectable people at the time of Jesus. Luke's Gospel tells of Jesus' encounters with two such shunned people – Zacchaeus, a social polluter, and the haemorrhaging woman (Luke 8.43–8 and parallels), a physical polluter. Notice how both Zacchaeus and the woman are on the edge of the crowd, existing at the margins before being drawn centre-stage.

If we return to the situation of the lost son, we can see that he pollutes himself in two ways. He has sexual relations with prostitutes, and he associates with pigs (and by implication, their dirt), itself indicative of commercial and cultural contamination. (Notice the link between pigs and the Roman 'Legion' of demons in the account of the Gerasene demoniac in Mark 5.) In these respects the young man's situation exactly parallels that of Jesus' sinful friends. By giving details of actions that so dramatically transgressed and offended the cultural norms of Jesus' first hearers, the story of the lost son makes it clear that he is not just geographically distant from his father's home but that he too is marginalized, having effectively banished himself. How has he ended up in this situation?

Initially perhaps he may have been drawn forward by simple hedonism, the desire to satisfy his appetite for pleasure, or perhaps a desire to break free from the restrictions of home and establish his own independent identity. So, either from thoughtlessness or from malice, we are not told, he travels far away and spends all his money with the single goal of satisfying what he takes to be his needs. Then something happens that is not his fault. A natural disaster strikes. This is a very important ingredient in the story because it is the occasion of the son's salvation. We shall examine the young man's response to famine in some detail using insights from the psychological 'Coping Theory'.[4]

The young man is in a stressful situation. There is no food in the land and he is therefore in danger of dying of starvation. We are told that he is in great need. In order to cope with this situation he needs to appraise the threat that it poses ('primary appraisal') and he needs to appraise the material and psychological resources at his disposal to meet this threat ('secondary appraisal'). We can infer that his primary appraisal of his situation is that it is grave and that the secondary appraisal is that his resources are negligible. He has no money to buy food. He has no local family from whom he can obtain food. But there is something he can do (a 'coping response' he can select) – he can attach himself to someone who has the power to provide for him. The text is clear here. The verb *kollaomai* means to 'unite oneself with' or to 'stick like glue to' (indeed it is often used to describe sexual relationships, as in Matthew 5.19 and 1 Corinthians 6.16). The young man chooses a coping response that is essentially a type of 'attachment behaviour', a phenomenon that we have already encountered in Chapter 4. There we saw that attachment to another person can bring emotional comfort. But if the one to whom we attach ourselves is powerful and strong then we are also literally strengthened by the association, and better equipped to face the world.

Attachment behaviour is especially useful in situations where we are weak and powerless. That is why it is so characteristic of small children and of people at times of stress. Research on the psychological reaction to trauma and life adversity suggests that this tendency contributes to the greater openness to spirituality that is often seen in the aftermath of terrible events – people express a desire to attach themselves to 'something greater'.[5]

It is thus natural and understandable that the prodigal son engages in attachment behaviour when faced with a crisis and few personal resources with which to meet it. His problem is, of course, that he chooses the wrong object for his attachment. In attaching himself to a 'citizen of that country' he makes precisely the same strategic mistake that the tax collectors and prostitutes have made in attaching themselves to the powerful oppressors of their people. It seems like a good idea, but it lands him in much worse trouble. For nobody actually gives him anything to eat. He is, after all, only hired out to a citizen of that country, not a citizen himself. His rejection of his father and his involvement with prostitutes had arisen from a desire to satisfy his appetites and aspirations at all costs. His involvement with a foreigner and his unclean animals arises from his attempts to remedy a bad situation, and they only compound it. The famine is not his fault, but the response it evokes in him shows just how low he has sunk.

The young man is living with the pigs, but his attachment to their owner has not had the intended effect of filling his belly. He is desperately hungry and has used up all his options. The image of the pig muck reminds us that he is dirty, but also that he is stuck. He is personally as well as financially spent. There are no coping responses left. This sort of situation has been described by Kenneth Pargament as 'the edge of efficacy'.[6] Noting the empirical research we quoted above on reaction to trauma, he argues that it is in situations like this that true religion can grow. In Chapter 3 we saw that the parables lead us intellectually into boundary situations that can challenge us and offer us glimpses of the kingdom of God. In the same way, real-life boundary situations, where we are on the edge, desperate because our own resources are depleted or spent, can allow us to let God in.

This is an important point. Very often this phenomenon is denigrated. People only turn to God when they are in trouble and ignore him when life is going well. The churches are full at times of national disasters such as 9/11, but otherwise are empty, and so on. But this is the nature of human spirituality, and it is passed over without condemnation or even comment in this parable. The essential feature of human turning or awakening to God is a realization that we are in need, that our own resources have let us down, and that other attachment objects don't work.

Turning

Only when things have got about as bad as they can get does the young man 'come to himself'. (This is the literal translation of the Greek phrase usually rendered 'came to his senses' in English.) What does this involve?

First, there is a remembering of something better, and with this a flicker of hope. Then there is a realistic appraisal of the situation, 'I am dying of hunger'. And on the basis of the memory from the past, a plan of action is formed. Finally the plan is enacted. There is a lot going on here that will repay careful examination.

We will work through this process, beginning with the young man's clearly stated intentions and their enactment, before exploring where these intentions really come from. Over the last 30 years social psychologists have demonstrated a very simple truth: if you want to predict how people will behave in a given situation, ask them what they intend to do. On the basis of these findings the 'Theory of Planned Behaviour' states that human beings 'are usually quite rational and make systematic use of the information available to them' when making immediate decisions about how to act, rather than being controlled by 'unconscious motives or over-powering desires', and that they 'consider the implications of their actions before they decide to engage or not engage in a particular behavior'.[7] An intention to act in a certain way is usually formulated on the basis of the action's estimated effectiveness in attaining a desired goal, its social acceptability, and the ease with which it can be performed.

The stories of the lost son and the dishonest manager furnish us with plenty of material in this area. We have a window into their minds because they engage in 'deliberative monologues' – they think aloud. The lost son plans a course of action. First, he judges that the goal of satisfying his hunger would be attained if he were to return to live in his father's house. His attitude towards this behaviour is positive. However, he knows that, given his track record, the behaviour is likely to be unacceptable to the household, especially his father. He comes up with a compromise solution: going home but presenting himself in a way that may be acceptable to his father using a formulaic expression of repentance. This would not be an easy course of action. He would lose face, be humiliated, and he might be turned away. But he still appraises it as a practical option – something he is capable of doing. This is for two motivational reasons, one obvious to him, one not quite conscious: his physical hunger, and his longing to go home. He needs food but he also needs his father. He forms his intention and he acts.

As the young man has pondered on this situation, crucially in the context of 'coming to himself', he has not said, 'I am hungry – what shall I do about it?' Rather, he has mused on what it is like to be at home and compared his present situation to this. It is as if he could only truly recognize his hunger when he related it to his memory of a place where people are satisfied. St Augustine envisages his remembering:

How then am I to seek for you, Lord? When I seek for you, my God, my quest is for the happy life . . . How then shall I seek for the happy life? . . . is it by remembering, as if I had forgotten it and still recall that I had forgotten? . . . My inquiry is whether this knowing is in the memory because, if it is there, we had happiness once . . . Surely this is not the way in which we recall joy? Well, perhaps it is. For even when sad, I remember my times of joy, like a wretched person thinking of the happy life . . . See how widely I have ranged, Lord, searching for you in my memory. I have not found you outside it . . . And so, since the time I learnt of you, you remain in my consciousness, and there I find you when I recall you and delight in you. These my holy delights you have given me, in your mercy looking upon my poverty.[8]

The theory of planned behaviour describes goal-directed action well. But its proponents admit that it stops short of addressing the origin of particular goals or attitudes in detail. What is the origin of this young man's positive attitude to returning home? Despite appearances, he has not forgotten his father's house. In his hunger, he recalls that there is food aplenty there. And so the goal of 'satisfying my hunger' starts to develop into 'going home in order to satisfy my hunger', with 'going home' definitely a subsidiary objective. Yet the influences on our life goals are not always fully conscious to us, and the going home part of the package is more important than it seems. The young man is coming to himself and is starting to realize that he belongs at home. This is not a repressed 'unconscious motive' in the psychoanalytic sense. Rather this homing tendency has, as it were, been on the back burner for some time and hunger has turned the heat up. The need for food is the immediate precipitant which starts to lay bare a deeper need – a need for belonging and restored relationships.

The link between hunger for life-giving bread and hunger for God is so characteristic of the teaching of Jesus, and ubiquitous in the Gospels, that it hardly needs to be spelt out here. Nevertheless, we should pause to reflect that hunger for bread is not just a convenient way of talking about hunger for God. These two types of hunger seem to be intrinsically connected, and come together in the person of Jesus. In the sixth chapter of John's Gospel, Jesus describes himself as living bread. The association of bread with Jesus is crucial in Luke's Gospel too, as we shall see in Chapter 10. The lost son was led astray by a desire, masquerading as a need, for something more exotic and pleasurable than bread. But he has come to the realization that his real need, the attraction of home and family, is for the nourishment that only something as basic as bread can give. It is also the dawning recognition that to become fully himself he must be on a homeward trajectory.

So many things, some at the forefront of our minds, others less obvious, influence the goals that direct our behavioural trajectories in this life. Arguably the strongest influence is a sense of our own identity (either corporate or individual), which in its turn depends on being in particular *relationships*. Where the goals that we pursue are concordant with an authentic sense of who we are we feel comfortable and fulfilled. Where they are at odds with our sense of identity we feel alienated, driven and stressed. The lost son may at first have thought that staying at home on his father's estate was beneath him, and would compromise his aspiration to be a man of the world. At the lowest point in the story he has lost his humanity and taken on the characteristics of an animal, with an animal's goals – the desire to eat the pods. As he comes to himself even the position of hired workers in his father's home, who at least have some human dignity, has become more attractive. It is more concordant with his emerging proper sense of self.

So, the things that feed his intention to arise and turn homewards are the desperation of his situation, a remembrance of, and then aspiration towards, a better time and place, and a growing awareness that he actually belongs in that place. Personality psychologist Kennon Sheldon comments that 'non-concordant individuals' who become trapped in 'unsatisfying ways of living' do so because they 'are doing the only thing they know how to do' and perhaps because they are 'afraid of change'. He continues, 'Initiating a life-transformation may require much energy and optimism, which the person may not be able to generate because of his or her current mode of functioning . . .'[9] The lost son has just enough energy, driven as he is by hunger, and just enough optimism as he remembers his father, to turn and take the first step home. Nothing more is required of him.

The Greek word *metanoia*, so often translated 'repentance', and associated with guilt and remorse, is perhaps better understood as a 'turning' or change of direction. In this story we are not told how guilty the son felt when he considered all that he had done to hurt his father and betray his people. We are not told that deep remorse led him to confess his sins with sincerity and weeping (though it is made clear that he was at some level aware that he had sinned). We are told that he felt hungry, remembered his father, and decided to turn around and go home.

Christian repentance is traditionally understood as turning from sin and towards Christ, a turning from goals that are discordant with our true selves and towards the goals of the kingdom (a rediscovery of the image of God that has been all the time hidden within us). This is perhaps what Jesus means when he talks about losing oneself in order to find oneself (for example Matthew 16.25). A simple turning is the beginning of transformation.

This turning can be seen in the drawing near of those wrong people to Jesus, in Zacchaeus' decision to climb a tree so that he could catch sight of Jesus, and in the touching of the hem of Jesus' garment by the haemorrhaging woman. These people were perhaps attracted by a rumour of hope, by someone who taught and acted as if things 'do not always have to be this way' and who evoked a kind of remembrance that they haven't always been this way. In theological terms the decision to turn, the forming of the intention to act, is the beginning of faith. It is based on hope, often desperate, and a memory, often faint, of the God who loves us unconditionally and awaits our response.

6

The meeting

---•◆•---

But while he was still far off his father saw him. He was moved
with pity, ran to him, embraced, and kissed him. The son said to
him, 'Father, I have sinned against heaven and in your sight; I am
no longer worthy to be called your son.' But his father said to his
slaves, 'Quickly, bring the best robe and put it on him, put a ring on
his finger and sandals on his feet. Bring the fatted calf and kill it.
Let us have a feast and celebrate. For this son of mine was dead and
is alive again, he was lost and has been found.' And they began to
celebrate.   (*Luke 15.20b–24*)

The young man has turned, arisen, and is making his way home,
but he still has a good way to go before he reaches his father's
house. However, he does not have far left to travel on his own. The
loneliness he must have felt in the distant country is about to come
to an end. His carefully thought-out plan of action is hijacked
before it can be completed. Indeed the whole focus of the story
has shifted. We are told no more of the son's feelings, motives and
thoughts. Instead there is a deceptively spare description of the
perception, emotion and action of the father. The father sees, feels
and runs. We shall consider each of these in turn, and we shall see
that they are each highly expressive of the father's *attitude*. This
attitude is love.

Seeing

The son is still far away when the father sees him. In order to detect
someone who is coming from far away you have to be looking in
the right direction. In order to identify him at this distance you
have to know him well and be expecting, hoping or fearing to see

him. So the phrase 'his father saw him' implies that he had an expectation or hope of seeing his son and that he was looking. In other words, he was watching and waiting.

What does watching expectantly mean? First of all it means being alert and awake, ready for action. Second, it means focusing attention towards the thing one is hoping to detect, tuning one's 'perceptual system' so that it readily responds to certain key features. The woman searching for the coin not only has to move obstacles and cover the whole area where the coin might possibly have fallen; she must also be attuned to the glint of metal. In the same way the man searching for his sheep must be on the alert for a glimpse of white or a faint bleat. The father in this story has likewise primed his search engine. He detects his son on the basis of minimal sensory evidence because he is expecting him and because he knows what to look for. He knows what to look for – most probably a characteristic gait pattern – because he knows his son.

Knowing and recognition are key aspects of the encounter between son and father in this story. The Bible also describes these as key aspects of the encounter between God and his people, and between the individual believer and God. Psalm 139 expresses wonder and awe at the possibility that humans can be known intimately by God. In his first letter to the Corinthians Paul remarks almost in passing about his experience of being fully known by God, and in his letter to the Galatians he reminds his readers that in becoming children of God they have essentially come to be *known by* God rather than to know God (1 Corinthians 13.12; Galatians 4.9). Having a sense of being truly known and understood is one of the most affirming experiences a human being can undergo. For this reason counsellors and psychotherapists aspire to such understanding together with the ability to communicate it to their clients – 'accurate empathy'.[1] John's Gospel tells us that both Nathanael and the Samaritan woman at the well were astonished and delighted at Jesus' knowledge of them (John 1.49, 50; John 4.29). Later in that Gospel Jesus himself talks about knowing his sheep (John 10.14). In Luke's Gospel we have the encounter with Zacchaeus. Jesus *looked* at Zacchaeus in the tree and he identified him. He knew where he was, and he called him by name.

The father hoped to see his son, but he did not know when he was coming, nor could he be certain that he would come at all. (This uncertainty is also intrinsic to the man's search for his sheep that we considered in Chapter 3.) The fact that the father spotted his son so quickly and easily, after a long period of separation and at a distance, tells us that he was maintaining a constant state of vigilance. Being chronically alert for a low-frequency, difficult-to-detect event is extremely difficult and exhausting. It is only worth the effort if the event is of great significance (for example, being on the lookout for icebergs when sailing in Arctic waters). From this alone we can conclude that the return of his son was of pre-eminent importance to the father.

Watching and waiting in this way is a form of seeking, but it involves very different behaviour from the wide-ranging expedition of the man seeking his sheep, or the frenetic search of the woman for her coin. In contrast to their activity, the father in this story seems strangely passive. This apparent passivity is there at the beginning, when he gives in without a murmur to his son's request for his inheritance in advance.

What is he up to? Why does he let his son take advantage of him in this way? Is he weak, naive, does he have some sort of need to be the victim? Robert Martin Walker's amusing 'Politically Correct' version of this story hits the nail on the head. The father's actions are described as 'dysfunctional' and 'codependent' by his older son, and he responds, 'I'm aware of my condition. I was victimized by a sobriety-deprived parent.' We are told that his son 'immediately made an appointment for his father with a therapist specializing in codependency'.[2] (In this context 'codependency' refers to a relationship where the abuser and the abused mutually support each other's dysfunctional behavioural patterns as ways of meeting their respective needs.)

Yet these questions, 'What is he up to? Why does he let them take advantage of him in this way? Is he weak, naive, does he have some sort of need to be the victim?' have a familiar feel. They are precisely the questions that troubled the disciples at the arrest of Jesus and its aftermath (Luke 22.49; 24.19–21), that seemed to trouble Pontius Pilate (John 19.10), and that still trouble some today. The key to understanding the apparent passivity of the father in this story is in fact the *passion* of Jesus. (The word 'passion' comes from the Latin word to experience or undergo, whether experiencing emotions – passions – or suffering. At the heart of the passion is Jesus' passivity in undergoing what happened to him.)

The motives of the father of the lost son remain largely hidden and must be inferred indirectly. We infer that the father suffers separation distress, hurt and rejection when his son goes away by his joy when his son returns. We infer that his passivity at the beginning of this story is more apparent than real by his alertness in watching for his son, and his dramatic rush to seize the initiative when he finally sees him. This is a father who knows when to wait and when to act, when to be silent and when to speak. In this he resembles Jesus, the active proclaimer of God's kingdom and the passive, silent victim of crucifixion. But, as we noted in Chapter 4, unlike this father the thoughts and feelings of Jesus are recorded for us in the Gospels: we do not have to infer them. Jesus wept over his rejection by Jerusalem, and as his passion began he struggled with a terrible dilemma: should he act or should he do nothing and let events take their course?

The anguish of Jesus in Gethsemane arose in the context of what was essentially an option appraisal. When faced with the threat of imminent arrest and no chance of a fair trial there are two obvious options: stay and fight, or turn and run. Both have a good chance of preserving one's life. In a similar way, when the father in this story is faced with the outrageous demand made by his younger son there are two obvious options: cast him out, or force him to comply with the demands of family duty. Both have a good chance of preserving one's dignity and fortune. But there is a third way. This is the 'do nothing' option.

There is a difference, though it may be difficult to detect on superficial inspection, between being frozen in anxious indecision amid two obvious options and actively choosing to embrace an alternative 'do nothing' option. The accounts of the agony in Gethsemane make it very clear that Jesus made an active choice of this sort, and that this was in response to his perception that to do nothing was the only viable way forward. He did not just, as it were, roll over. He chose to stay put and let events take their course.

Jesus' dialogue with his heavenly Father is prefigured by the temptation narratives (Luke 4.1–13 and parallels). In the desert Jesus was faced with choices centred on the use of power. He could use his power to meet his physical needs, to test the relationship of trust with his Father and, of most importance in the present context, to dominate, control and subdue the peoples of the world. But Jesus' mission was all about love. There is no room in a love relationship for domination, control and subjugation. Love is about allowing the other person to respond freely, not coerced, not bribed, and not seduced by dazzling signs.

So, intrinsic to Jesus' love mission to the world was the risk of cruel rejection, and as the events in the Garden of Gethsemane unfolded it became clear that this risk was about to be realized. To continue in obedience to his Father's agenda of love entailed neither tactical withdrawal nor defensive resistance, but active compliance with the act of rejection. This is a terrible truth, difficult for the human mind to comprehend (Mark 8.32, 33; John 18.36), and evidently deeply distressing to Jesus himself.

In his classic book *The Stature of Waiting*, W. Vanstone explores this challenging theme in some depth, drawing principally on the Gospels of Mark and John. From these texts he draws out the transition from working to waiting, from physical freedom to physical constraint, from action to passion, in the last week of Jesus' life.[3] Most tellingly, he observes that in the sentences of Mark's Gospel Jesus ceases to be the grammatical subject and becomes the object – he no longer does things, they are done to him – and he argues that for the first Christians this compliance with rejection expressed in being 'handed over' was as central to the story of salvation as was the crucifixion itself. This is evident in a number of texts, which all use the verb *paradidomi* (see Acts 3.13; Romans 8.32; 1 Corinthians 11.23; Galatians 2.20; Ephesians 5.2), variously translated as 'betrayed', 'gave' or 'delivered up', but which in its essence means being passed from one person to another.

Like Jesus, the father in this story actively complies with an act of rejection. He may have been tempted to cast out his son, thus satisfying his anger, or to keep him close and force him to work for him under tough conditions, thus consolidating his assets. But neither alternative would have enabled the development or restoration of a love relationship. Indeed they almost guarantee the establishment of a hate relationship. They are rejected because this father's main concern is not his money, his dignity or his power; it is the love of his son. His son is not a coin or a sheep that can simply be picked up and carried home. He is an adult human being who has the capacity to turn homewards himself. In the economy of love the father must wait for this turning before he moves to offer the welcome that has been in his heart from the beginning.

The interlocked relationship between 'passive' waiting and active welcome in the life of Jesus is poignantly and significantly expressed in Luke's passion narrative. Jesus hangs on the cross, to all appearances passively waiting to die. The passers-by and soldiers each reprise the option appraisal he has already gone through in Gethsemane, taunting him by suggesting he acts to save himself and confirm his identity as the Messiah. One of the other crucified thieves hanging beside him joins in. But the other thief turns, about as late in the day as it is possible to turn, and at his lowest ebb, and asks Jesus to remember him, to *know him again*. And, like the running father, Jesus assures him not only of recognition, but of a place at the heavenly feast.

Feeling

The father sees something coming towards him in the distance and recognizes it as his son. And now we have the first direct indication of the father's feelings. He is 'moved with pity'. The Greek verb here, *esplagkhnisthe*, is a term we have already come across in Chapter 4 in the context of Jesus' encounter with the widow of Nain (Luke 7.13). This is a word that is at once biological and divine in tone. It refers to the physical seat of the emotions – in modern idiom the heart, in ancient idiom the guts, in the English of King James the bowels. In the Bible it is specifically used to refer to the loving kindness and mercy of God and the compassion of Jesus. It carries with it the feeling of longing and yearning. In the

Gospels of Matthew and Mark it is used to describe Jesus' feeling as he surveyed the crowds who came to him in need (Matthew 9.35; 14.14; Mark 8.2).

As Jesus sees human beings in material and spiritual need he is deeply moved. As this father sees his son at the end of his resources he too is deeply moved. The story of how the situation arose is not relevant at this moment. All that matters is the drawing near of needy people who recognize their need. The response is unmitigated compassion.

Again, we have a picture of God painted in emotional colours. It is made very clear that the subsequent actions of the father have strong affective overtones. He has not made a measured, calculated decision to try again in his relationship with his son. Rather, his behaviour is the natural partner of his feelings. It is not measured at all. It is rapid, energized and extreme.

Running

Kenneth Bailey's study of this story has highlighted the counter-cultural nature of the running father. He draws on both ancient Near Eastern literature and his observation of contemporary rural Arab life to illustrate this point:

> A pastor of my acquaintance was not accepted as the pastor of a particular church because, in the judgment of the elders, he walked down the street too fast.[4]

In this analysis, running to meet his son brings with it an unthinkable loss of dignity and honour to the father. Some scholars speculate that such a man could only have been induced to run in this way to protect his son from dangerous hostility on the part of local people. But the text says nothing about this. It says that the father saw his son, was moved with pity, and ran.

Carol Schestern LaHurd's study of contemporary Arab Christian women challenges the 'unthinkable' nature of the running father.[5] The women she interviewed expressed no surprise at all at such a notion, and explained it as a natural welcoming back of one's own blood. LaHurd perceptively notes what many contemporary anthropologists have also discovered. Societal norms and written codes may not tell us as much as we think about how real people in these societies actually behave. There are times when such norms will be transgressed, especially where intimate relationships and high emotion are involved.

It is therefore not so much the running that is remarkable as the welcome that it represents. The son's behaviour would definitely have been unacceptable in his culture. Welcoming a returning son home by running to meet him may have been somewhat unusual. But welcoming *this* son home is indeed extraordinary.

The father's behaviour has an impulsive, almost irrational, quality to it that has troubled some commentators. Yet contemporary philosophical reflections on the nature of morality and ethics have advanced the view that truly moral actions are essentially of this sort. They are not thought out, not rule-bound, and are not conditional on the behaviour of the other person:

> The moral call is thoroughly personal; it appeals to my responsibility, and the urge to care thus elicited cannot be allayed or placated by the awareness that others do it for me, or that I have already done my share by following to the letter what others used to do . . . If rules are missing, however, my plight is harder, since I cannot gain reassurance by faithfully following standards I can observe in others, memorize and imitate . . . I am moral *before* I think. There is no thinking without concepts . . . , standards . . . , rules . . . But when concepts, standards, and rules enter the stage moral impulse makes an exit . . .[6]

This father has plenty of slaves, but he does not send them out to meet his son while he composes himself at home. (In this he is like the man who does not delegate the search for his lost sheep.) He will not have forgotten his son's transgressions, he will know that he has already been more than generous to his son and could legitimately say that he has done all that could be done, and he will be aware that it is generally considered undignified for a man in his position to run. But he sees his son, is gutted, and runs. In this story and in his own actions Jesus tells us something profound about the moral character of God.

The father's attitude – his enduring disposition – towards his son is one of love. God's attitude towards his people is one of love. This is primarily a moral rather than an emotional characteristic, but it is expressed and experienced both in this story, and in the lives of believers, in deeply emotional terms; in feelings of compassion, hugs and kisses, and joy.

The embrace

The father's running culminates in an embrace and a kiss. As the son slowly draws near to the father, the father quickly covers a good distance and meets him face to face. This coming close can be seen as the fulfilment of the moral impulse that made the father run. Indeed, the postmodern philosopher Emmanuel Levinas has described morality in terms of 'proximity'. The core of this moral proximity is a suppression of the distance between two persons, the establishment or affirmation of the obligation of one to the other, forgetting 'reciprocity as in love that does not expect to be shared'.[7]

This characteristic offering of himself in love without expectation can be seen in the structure of the father's embrace of the son. It is important to notice that this embrace is not described as mutual, like the running into each other's arms of Hollywood lovers. The father embraces his son. The action of embrace can be broken down into four parts: opening arms, waiting, closing arms, and re-opening arms.[8]

The opening of arms in embrace signifies a welcome for the other, the making of an opening in one's personal space to let him in. It is an active invitation, offering a place to the other person and rendering oneself vulnerable to rejection or attack (see for example 2 Samuel 29.9–10). It signifies unconditional acceptance.

Next comes a period of waiting, perhaps only fleeting, perhaps lasting several seconds. For the father in this story this is a reiteration of his long period of awaiting his son's return. The waiting is necessary because without it the embrace would be a rapacious seizure. Some glimmer of response from the other must be observed before the embrace can proceed. Welcoming touch is offered rather than imposed. This echoes the gospel accounts of Jesus' attitude towards healing touch. The gospel writers do not tell us that he ran around Galilee indiscriminately touching any sick people he encountered. In general he is described as responding to the approaches of sick people or their advocates. Only then does he touch.[9] Sometimes this point is laboured, for instance in the story of the blind beggar (Luke 18.41).

The embrace is consummated with the closing of the arms. Having given his implicit consent, the lost son is held in safety and intimacy by his father. The wrong attachment behaviour of the son is superseded by the right attachment behaviour of the father. There is a move from the affirmation of being known to that of being taken hold of, an experience to which Paul refers, again almost in passing, in Philippians 3.12. The son is contained and sheltered by the father's arms, like the chicks under the wings of the mother hen. His sins too, evident in the dirt that still clings to him, are covered. Psalm 32, which anticipates the story of the lost son, gives a moving account of this experience. It is a psalm that seems to have been important to Paul as he reflected on the human situation and its need for redemption (Romans 4.7).

This whole experience of being held, contained and covered is expressed by Paul in spiritual terms as being 'in Christ'. In 2 Corinthians 5 he reflects on what this means for the believer. It means being who you were meant to be – a child of God whose goal is to live for Christ, part of a new creative process. It means being reconciled to God through God's reconciling action in Christ, through his choosing not to count people's sins against them. And, exactly as in the case of Zacchaeus, it means becoming an agent for reconciliation oneself (2 Corinthians 5.15–21).

The watching, waiting, running and embracing of the father in this story are all pictures of God's redeeming love expressed in his coming into the world in Jesus. They are unexpected, costly, risky, precisely timed, and they signify forgiveness. At the end of his discussion of being in Christ, Paul says a strange thing: 'He made the one who knew no sin to be sin for our sake, so that in him we might become the righteousness of God' (2 Corinthians 5.21). How is this relevant to being in Christ? How does it connect with the lost son as he is held by his father?

The answer is that, as we discussed at some length in Chapter 5, this young man returns home dirty and contaminated. He is smelly and ritually unclean. He should have washed himself before approaching his father. Yet his father hugs him, kisses him and throws his arms around him. In doing this the father is contaminated, and the contamination of the son is covered. The one who was clean becomes dirty and the one who was dirty is, by association, cleansed.

Again, we see this played out in the life of Jesus (and, Paul argues, supremely in his death and resurrection). Jesus touched people who were polluters. He touched lepers, he was touched by the haemorrhaging woman. These people were healed and saved, and Jesus was fully open to contamination by them. This too is one of the concerns of the Pharisees in commenting on Jesus' close association with the 'wrong' sorts of people. Yet Jesus was not diminished by his contact with disease and impurity. Immediately after being touched by the haemorrhaging woman we are told that he went straight on without washing and brought healing, not pollution, to Jairus' daughter (Luke 8.48, 49). And Jesus was in no way diminished by his passion nor held by death.

The final stage of embrace is the reopening of the arms. The other has not been engulfed by the embrace, has not been absorbed into the identity of the embracer, but is free to be himself. Yet the fact that the embrace has taken place gives security, an authentic attachment from which to move forward in confidence. And it is at this point, when he has received *unconditional* acceptance, that the son, who had seen his confession as a *condition* of future acceptance, actually makes his confession.

The beginning of transformation

The son remembered his father and turned homewards. His father ran to him and offered an embrace. The son assented to the embrace and thus participated in it. There is a sense in which he surrendered himself to the love of his father. His behaviour then started to change. Through the ages this has been a recurring theme in the experience of individuals as they encounter the love of God in Christ. This may be a particular feature of initial 'conversion' experiences, but it is also a characteristic of the continuing turning and meeting Jesus that forms part of Christian discipleship.

This process begins with some sense, however small, of dissatisfaction with the way things are. Alongside this there is a kind of seeking, or perhaps remembering, which may be barely conscious. Then comes an encounter with the risen Christ. Whatever form that takes, from the direct and dramatic to the subtle and oblique, there is a recognition that this is a meeting with a real historical person who once met people in the towns and villages of Galilee.[10] The experience of this encounter includes a sense of forgiveness or release, and often involves something like self-surrender. This surrender results in behaviour change, particularly in the area of personal morality:

> Each little step towards the centre seemed like an impossible demand, a demand requiring me to let go one more time from wanting to be in control, to give up one more time the desire to predict life, to die one more time to the fear of not knowing where it all will lead, and to surrender one more time to the love that knows no limits. And still, I knew that I would never be able to live the great commandment to love without allowing myself to be loved without conditions or prerequisites.[11]

Excellent descriptions of the process of transforming encounter with God in Christ can be found in William James' historical study of dramatic conversion experiences. A more temperate account is given by C. S. Lewis in his story of his own journey to faith.[12] But Luke himself furnishes us with several case studies.

First there is Zacchaeus, a dissatisfied man, seeking Jesus, called by name, welcomed unconditionally with joy and celebration, who then changes his behaviour and treats other people with generosity in response to the generosity he himself has experienced.

Then there is Saul, a very dissatisfied man who persecutes the Christians. The Greek word for 'persecute', *dioko*, also means to 'pursue'. Saul pursues the Christians and he pursues Christ. He meets Christ Jesus, is called by name, and all his later writings tell of the loving embrace he experienced. His behaviour changes so dramatically that it creates natural suspicion. In Luke's account of Saul's conversion we are also told something else. Jesus tells Saul that he has been 'kicking against the goads' (Acts 26.14). He is talking about 'non-concordant' behaviour. Like the lost son, Saul is engaging in actions which go directly against who he is truly meant to be. This is the final key component of meeting with Jesus. We start to find and to become our authentic self.

Finally there is Simon Peter, a man who is called by Jesus, travels alongside him, but takes a long time to 'see' Jesus (Luke 9.18–36). He is one of his key followers who falls away (Luke 22.61–2), and is at his lowest ebb, before he turns back again (Luke 22.31, 32). He meets Jesus once more (Luke 24.34), presumably experiences forgiveness and, even before the dramatic events of Pentecost, his behaviour changes. In Luke's account of the life of Peter we see something of the ebb and flow of Christian discipleship, of encounter and re-encounter with Jesus, of turning to him and returning to him, of forgiveness once and forgiveness again. By all accounts Peter did not find it easy to follow Jesus. In many ways his call went against the grain (see also Acts 11). Yet there are indications that he too found his true self only in Christ. John's Gospel recounts that many disciples found Jesus' message too hard to stomach. Jesus asks Peter if he also wishes to leave him and Peter replies, 'Lord, who can we go to? You have the words of eternal life' (John 6.68). Despite the enormous difficulties along the way, alluded to again in John 21.18, Peter felt that following Jesus was the only authentic option available to him. He also loved him deeply, and that helped!

7

Envy and forgiveness

————•◆•————

Now his elder son was going about on the farm; yet when he drew
near to the house, he heard music and dancing. He summoned
one of the servants and asked him what was going on. He replied,
'*Your brother* has come, and *your father* has killed the fatted calf,
because he has got him back safe and sound.' Then he became
angry and refused to go in. His father came out and began to plead
with him. But he answered his father, 'Listen! For so many years
I have worked *like a slave* for you and I have never broken any of
your rules; yet you have never given me even a young goat for a
party with my friends. But when *this son of yours* turns up, who has
devoured your property with prostitutes, you killed the fatted calf
for him!' Then he said to him, '*Child*, you have always been with
me, and all that is mine is yours. But we had to celebrate and
rejoice, because *this brother of yours* was dead and has come to life;
he was lost and has been found.'   (*Luke 15.25–32*)

The story of the father and his younger son may seem to have
ended 'happily ever after', but the parable began with the words
'There was a man with two sons'; what of the other son? So far he
has been absent from the story. One might even say ignored. We
find him working in the fields, going about his, and indeed his
father's, business, as he has done for many years. There doesn't
even seem to have been a messenger sent to invite him to the party.
The Greek words can be understood to indicate that he was going
about his business and just happened to draw near to the house.
Then he hears the party. Intrigued, he finds out what is going on
but does not like what he hears. He reminds us of the scribes and
Pharisees. They too were 'going about their business', indeed, as
we have seen, taking seriously God's (their Father's) business in

the villages of Galilee. They must have kept coming across the crowds and commotion which surrounded Jesus. 'What is going on?' would be a natural question to ask. The problem was the answer: 'Jesus is welcoming and eating with the tax collectors and sinners.' For the elder son in this story the problem is also about the welcome of a sinner.

The language used to describe the relationships between the father and his sons in this section of the story is significant (the key words are highlighted in the passage above). The servant uses the terms 'your brother' and 'your father' when describing to the elder son what has happened. In a sense this is unsurprising – what other terms would the servant use? Nevertheless it emphasizes that the three belong to the same family. It reminds us of the context in which the behaviour of the elder son arises.

We are told that the elder son becomes 'angry'. Psychological and anthropological research indicates that the class of emotions that come under the umbrella of 'anger' in most cultures is generally evoked by *rule transgression*. Anger can be thought of as a 'social enforcement mechanism'.[1] But what rules have been transgressed? Has the elder son lost his inheritance? No – this is made clear when his father tells him 'all that is mine is yours'. All that he might have expected from his father will be his. What is troubling him is that he feels that his father has transgressed rules concerning his relationship with his other son. But this doesn't affect him directly – so why is he bothered?

The reaction of the older son contains both explicit objections to his father's conduct, and some implicit questions. These are essentially that his father's unconditional welcome of the prodigal calls into question

- the validity of his older son's obedience to social convention and family obligation
- his love for his older son
- his own honour.

Precise parallels to these questions are raised rhetorically and engaged with systematically by Paul in his letter to the Romans. Paul was writing about the issues raised for God's chosen people, the Jews, as 'sinful' Gentiles were welcomed into the Church on the basis of faith alone:

- What is the point of the law? (Romans 3.1, 2)
- Does God not love his people? (Romans 11.1)
- Does God dishonour himself? (Romans 3.3, 4, 21–6)

There are many such points of contact and resonances between the story of the prodigal son and his brother, and Paul's letter to the Romans. They repay further study in their own right. Paul the Pharisee engages seriously and sympathetically with Pharisaic concerns. But the story of the prodigal son meets these concerns in another way. There is a recognition that the objections to the welcoming in of sinners are not primarily theological or philosophical, but emotional – and can be framed as the questions, 'Does Dad love me?' and 'Is Dad's love worth having?'

The psychology of envy

Families are not collections of individuals who exist alongside each other, independently pursuing their own concerns. They involve complex networks of interconnected and dynamic relationships. What affects one will affect all. In his first letter to the Corinthians Paul uses the analogy of the body to apply this point to the Church (1 Corinthians 13.26). Individuals take on roles or positions in families. These roles are determined by a combination of factors including age, gender, temperament, family culture, and the impact of events. Sometimes individuals get trapped in set roles, sometimes the roles are more fluid. Within the family, individuals can form alliances with some and turn against others. Again, these alliances can be rigid or fluid. Families have histories and, when it comes to bearing grudges within the family, long memories.

In this story the elder son is the responsible one who has played things by the book. In this he conforms to all that we know about being the firstborn child in a family, both from academic research[2] and our own experience. In general, firstborn children are treated more strictly by their parents. The parenting of firstborn children can seem like a rehearsal for the main show. Firstborn children take on adult roles and responsibilities relatively early, and less allowance is made for their emotional needs. The typical grievance of the oldest child is one of under-appreciation by her parents. This is why the behaviour of the elder son has such an authentic feel, and why many of us who are eldest children experience a good degree of sympathy for him. He has kept the rules, and it has not been easy. His younger brother has flouted the rules, and has not only been let off, but has been treated with deep affection. If we can empathize at all with his feelings, it may help us to see the scribes' and Pharisees' horror at the actions of Jesus in a more kindly light. Indeed, this part of the story seems to be addressed, with some gentleness, particularly to them. It acknowledges the 'But it's not fair!' response, already touched on in Chapter 4, that we can feel when confronted with the boundless generosity of God's grace.

The identity of each of us is partly shaped and expressed by the roles and positions we take in our families: 'clown', 'carer', 'listener', 'provider', 'scapegoat', 'favourite', 'invalid', 'protector', and so on. But these roles are themselves defined as much by what they are not as by what they are. If I am the listener then I am not the talker. If I am the carer then I am not the one who is cared for. (How hard it is for people who have cared for others all their lives finally to accept care themselves!) A large part of being the elder child can be found in not being the younger child. The elder brother is the not-prodigal son as much as he is anything else. Note the contrast he draws between his brother and himself. He is the 'good boy' in the family, and his brother is the 'naughty boy'.

The shaping of both personal and group identity by being 'not' is a widely recognized psychological phenomenon.[3] I can be most truly me by defining myself in contrast to something else. There are strong hints of this in Jesus' exchange with his mother that we looked at in Chapter 4: '". . . your father and I have been anxiously searching for you . . ." ". . . Didn't you know that I had to be in my Father's house?"' (Luke 2.48–9). This emphasizes Jesus' divine sonship by setting it against the statement that he is Joseph's son. There is also a detailed consideration of this point in the story of the tax collector and the Pharisee (Luke 18.9–14). The Pharisee's sense of who he is in relation to God rests primarily on being unlike sinners, and only secondarily on his own actions.[4] In a similar way, many of the psalms explore the theme of what it means to be in a righteous relationship with God as much in terms of what it means to be in an unrighteous relationship with him. Psalm 1.1 sets the tone for much of the whole book: 'Happy are those who do not follow the advice of the wicked . . .'

As Christians we too construct our identity in this way over and against the world. But, like the Pharisees before us, we can be vulnerable to the tendency to over-emphasize difference as a basis for our identity. A casual entering of the terms 'Christian' and 'celebrate' into an internet search engine gives an interesting insight. Instead of items concerned with the celebration of the life, death and resurrection of Jesus, the coming of God's kingdom, or the Eucharist, we find items urging Christians *not* to celebrate Hallowe'en, or the overly commercialized festivals of Christmas and Easter, and even birthdays. In a society that is increasingly dominated by secular culture it is tempting to shore up our distinctive identity in terms of being not-like this culture rather than being like Christ. Thus we may give particular attention to things we don't believe in, for instance buying lottery tickets, reading horoscopes, shopping on a Sunday, or subscribing to satellite television. Strong beliefs about cultural pollution and contamination, and a tendency to separate ourselves from others by blaming them, are the natural consequence of a sense of identity whose dominant marker is difference from the other.

This story tells us nothing about the histories, temperaments and abilities of the two brothers, and we go beyond the text if we speculate about such things. What it does tell us is that the not-prodigal son is different from his brother in the life choices he has made. His actions form part of a life strategy that both flows from and consolidates his sense of himself as the 'good' or 'not-bad' boy. When we make such strategic choices in life they are based on some sort of option appraisal, however rudimentary. In choosing our favoured option we reject all the alternatives. Having reached a decision, we commit ourselves to a course of action, and with this comes a sense of responsibility.

But suppose we have made the wrong choice? Suppose the outcome of our decision is disappointing in some way? There is increasing evidence that disappointment is one of the most aversive experiences that humans can undergo. If the disappointment arises as a direct result of a decision a person himself has made it can be even more aversive, and may often be complicated by guilt or shame. It feels good to have moved into the fastest moving motorway lanes when traffic is congested. Conversely it feels miserable, frustrating and witless to have chosen a queue that has ground to a halt, and to watch traffic in the other lanes move relentlessly past. The same applies to supermarket checkout queues. It feels good to have bought the same computer model as our friend, but to have paid £100 less through a different dealer. It feels bad and embarrassing to have paid £100 more.

In modern consumer society the plethora of choice has paradoxically resulted in a decrease in life satisfaction.[5] One reason for this is that there are so many more opportunities for disappointment. 'Would I be happier if I had actually bought that car, chosen that wife, opted for that school for my children?' Because of the aversive nature of disappointment people go to great lengths to avoid it. The very process of reaching a decision is complicated by checking out multiple alternatives to ensure that we really are getting the best deal and will not be disappointed in our choice. Once we have made our choice and cannot go back, we may defend ourselves against feelings of disappointment through various processes of psychological appraisal. One of these is 'downward comparison'. This is where we make ourselves particularly aware of the negative effects of the choices we didn't make. By focusing on these negative effects, the attractiveness of our choice increases and its capacity to disappoint us decreases.

The elder son has chosen the 'good-boy' strategy. He does not enjoy his work for his father's business, he has not had as much fun as his brother, but at least he can console himself with the fact that his strategy will pay off. He has a secure inheritance and position. He surely has the approval of his father. His brother may have had fun, but it has taken him off the scene and alienated him from the family circle. Until the return of his brother he can tell himself

87

that his was a good choice because it was better than the alternative. He can make a downward comparison. But now it looks as if the younger son's choice has also paid off. Both strategies have resulted in an invitation to the party. Indeed the younger son is the guest of honour.

Even though the outcome for the not-prodigal is all that he could have expected, his own choice is now thrown into question. It seems that he is in deficit. The reason for this is simply that he has achieved the same outcome as his brother but has not had the same fun. Like the disappointed workers in the vineyard (Matthew 20.1–16), 'who have borne the burden of the day and the scorching heat', he responds with indignation. From his perspective his father's brand of justice is deeply unjust.

This makes it clear that a key goal of the elder brother's strategy in staying at home and working on his father's estate was what he could get out of it. If the work he was doing had any intrinsic reward, because it was fun, or because it expressed his feelings of love towards his father, he would not be in deficit in relation to his brother. If anything, he would have the advantage and could afford to be generous in his attitude. But he says that the work at home has been a kind of slavery (there is a resonance with Romans 7.14 here), a simple obedience to parental orders. 'I had been working very hard on my father's farm but had never really tasted the joy of being at home.'[6] He bemoans the lack of gifts from his father. Gifts are a sign of love. The elder son is not necessarily simply mercenary in his motives. His 'good-boy' strategy was aimed at earning something – certainly material wealth and security, but also, and perhaps more fundamentally and not fully consciously, his father's love and approval.

Thus the issue goes beyond the struggle of each brother for a sense of distinctive identity, expressed in the distinctive life strategies each has chosen. It goes beyond the respective success of these strategies. It is as much about what *each feels he is worth in the eyes of his father*, and hence in his own eyes. It is about self-worth or self-esteem.[7]

The elder son's self-worth is, like his identity, shaped by not being like his brother. He feels that he is more valuable to his father, more worthy of his father's love, because of his own good actions, which are thrown into relief by the despicable actions of his brother. We are all familiar with this sort of feeling, especially if we are somewhat insecure. We hear of the failings of our peers or of those to whom we aspire with mingled compassion and delight. The phenomenon of *Schadenfreude* – pleasure evoked by the misfortunes of others – is well known. It is exploited by the sort of celebrity gossip magazines that aim to please their readers by offering them pictures of glamorous stars of screen and sport looking fat, ugly and depressed. In a similar way we may be inexplicably cheered after spending time with friends who are in trouble – 'at least there's someone worse off than me'. Or we may feel inexplicably low when we hear of the success of others – even if their success is not at our own expense. The explanation for our feelings is that, in the light of the misfortunes of others, we have come to see ourselves as worth more, and in the light of their success we have come to see ourselves as worth less. It is easy for us to sympathize with the elder son for these reasons alone. The more worthless and unlovable his brother seems, the more worthwhile and lovable he feels.

This is one way of understanding the rivalry that is common between siblings. In the Old Testament the archetypal relationship between brothers is that of rivalry for the approval of God, rather than fraternal solidarity (Cain and Abel in Genesis 4). This is played out as rivalry between brothers for the approval and love of their father (Jacob and Esau in Genesis 27; Joseph and his eleven brothers in Genesis 37). In the story of the prodigal son the elder brother feels unloved and undervalued because his father seems to love and value his rival, a well-recognized psychological phenomenon termed 'sibling barricade'.[8] The father's embrace of one son is experienced as exclusion by the other.

In his anger and, we have argued, in his hurt the elder son turns *away* from the older man. In stark contrast to his returning brother, he does not address him as 'Father' even though the text makes it clear that this relationship still stands. It is sad to note that, even in his despair, the younger son thought that his father would treat him at least as 'one of the hired workers'; in contrast, in his anger, the elder son claims he has been treated 'like a slave'. He is invited into the house to join the party but he refuses to go in. Instead he attempts to justify himself by appealing to his scrupulous and joyless life of obedience to his father's commands and by pointing the finger at 'this son of yours' who, in his view, is not entitled to be there. Like the tax collectors and sinners who by their behaviour were seen to have placed themselves outside the covenant, in his view the prodigal son has placed himself outside the family circle.

One of the things that can boost our sense of self-worth is the feeling that we belong to an exclusive club. The club needs to have a small membership and the criteria for membership need to be recognized as worthwhile. It helps if we know that others would like to join this club and are disappointed that they cannot be admitted. If they start letting just anybody into these sorts of clubs we feel diminished because the club itself has been diminished:

> APRIL 30. Perfectly astonished at receiving an invitation for Carrie and myself from the Lord and Lady Mayoress to the Mansion House to 'meet the Representatives of Trades and Commerce'. My heart beat like that of a schoolboy. Carrie and I read the invitation over two or three times. I could scarcely eat my breakfast . . . MAY 3 . . . While speaking incidentally to Spotch, one of our head clerks, about the Mansion House, he said: 'Oh, I'm asked, but don't think I shall go.' When a vulgar man like Spotch is asked I feel my invitation is considerably discounted.[9]

Like Mr Pooter, the writer of this fictional *Diary of a Nobody* (another telling name), the elder son thinks his invitation to the party is considerably discounted. It is so discounted that it is worthless. The party is not worth attending.

And here we see again the multiple levels at which this parable can speak. It tells of the human relationship of two brothers. It tells of the tendency for individuals to become complacent, self-righteous and unforgiving, shoring up their self-esteem by focusing on the inferiority of others. It tells of the feelings of the Pharisees when faced with the welcome offered to tax collectors and prostitutes by Jesus. For Luke's first audience this parable would also have spoken powerfully about the relationship between the Jews and an emerging Church that welcomed Gentiles. Jesus' inclusion of the tax collectors and sinners leads as a natural consequence to the inclusion of the Gentiles. Once the barrier has been breached by the tax collectors and sinners, other people beyond the margins can flood in. This universal implication of Jesus' open welcome to table fellowship was something that was perhaps intuited and therefore feared by the Pharisees, but only became fully realized and was only fully understood by his disciples after his death (Acts 10.9–48).

The welcoming of Gentiles as the early Church spread raised enormous questions about God's relationship with his chosen people, the Jews. It also meant that from the perspective of faithful Jews the Church was essentially a party not worth attending. And if the party is not worth attending what does that say about the host?

Forgiveness and justice

The text makes it clear that the elder son's anger arises in the context of concern for his own well-being. But alongside this it is possible that there is a higher concern for the integrity and dignity of his father. This concern is certainly evoked in the reader. We have already explored the strange behaviour of the father earlier in the parable – his acquiescence to his young son, his passive watching and waiting, his undignified running, his close embrace of a person who is unclean. In welcoming his son home unconditionally it seems as if the father is not only doing an injustice to his elder son but also an injustice to himself, and is thus diminished. The elder son's indignation may reflect in part a desire to protect his father from ridicule, perhaps out of love, perhaps out of a wish to maintain his own social standing. In the same way the Pharisees may have thought that Jesus was bringing God into disrepute in his actions with sinners. They wanted to protect God.

Many commentators have identified similarities between the reuniting of the father and prodigal son whom he describes as 'dead', and the reuniting of Jacob with his lost son Joseph whom he had long presumed dead (Genesis 46.28–30). But there is a crucial difference. Joseph had triumphed in the far-off land of Egypt and his father's status could only have been enhanced as a result of their reconnection. In contrast the prodigal son returns home from the far country in disgrace, and surely this must have a negative impact on his father's status?

At the heart of this story of reconciliation between father and son is the covering of the younger son's dirty and damaged body by the embrace of his father. This is something that the twenty-first century reader might describe as forgiveness. It is easy to talk about forgiveness, indeed earlier in the Gospel Jesus has presented *aphesis* – a term usually translated 'forgiveness' – as a key feature of discipleship without much further comment (Luke 6.37; 11.4). But as anyone who has been deeply hurt but tried genuinely to forgive his abuser knows, the process of forgiveness is painful, unsettling and anxiety-provoking. This parable does not talk about the concept of forgiveness. The word *aphesis* is never mentioned. Instead it draws the reader in, so that he may identify with the father, sympathize with the older son, and thus both feel the discomfort and wrestle with the questions that forgiveness entails.

A common misinterpretation of forgiveness is that the person who forgives is stigmatized and disempowered. To forgive seems to entail a diminishing of identity. This is because in some way it means to acknowledge and accept the assault on one's person rather than to defend against it, to embrace the role of victim in relationship to a more powerful or controlling perpetrator. There are several ways that we can defend our sense of identity and personal control against the assaults of others. The first is by denying that we have been assaulted at all – 'Oh, it was nothing'. If there is no assault then there is no stigma. The second is defensive aggression – dishing it out as well as taking it, the seeking of retribution. The power imbalance between perpetrator and victim is rectified by proportional retribution, and the stigmatizing identity of victim is relinquished as she becomes in her turn a kind of perpetrator.

The third and most complex type of defence is self-blame – 'It must have been my fault'. In some ways this is also a type of denial. If the assault was my own fault then it was not so much an assault as a natural consequence of the sort of person I am. Paradoxically, it can be more acceptable to believe that I am worthless, and that events are usually my fault, than to accept that I have little control over the actions of others who compromise my identity by their assaults. Again, I avoid being a victim, but this time it is because I am the despicable author of my own fate. This last type of defence is commonly seen in both adults and children who have been in long-term abusive relationships that they have little or no power to change. It seems, by a compelling though twisted type of logic, that to retain some coherent sense of identity, to continue to believe that the universe is controllable, such people come to believe that what happens to them is largely their own fault. This thinking is often explicitly endorsed by the perpetrators of their abuse.

In the light of this we must be extraordinarily careful in apply-ing a spirituality of forgiveness. Forgiveness is *not* about saying 'Oh – it was really my fault, I'm sorry.' That may be a part of repen-tance. It is not forgiveness. It is very important to understand that when Jesus talks about forgiveness it is in the context of the more powerful person in a relationship forgiving a person who is in a less powerful position. Forgiveness is thus intimately connected with mercy. Sometimes it is hard to see who is in the position of power. In this parable it is the father who, at the point when he is in the position of emotional and material power, is doing the forgiving. In the parable of the unmerciful servant (Matthew 18.21f) it is the servant who is in the position of power who is required to release his colleague from his debts.

'Release' or 'cancel' is in fact another way of translating the word *aphesis* (see for instance Luke 4.18), and the New Testament understanding of forgiveness is at least as much about liberation from bondage as it is about exoneration from immorality. The person who is in a position to release from prison and to cancel debts is the person who is in the position of power. This gives us new insight into Jesus' words, 'Father, forgive them' as he hangs on the cross (Luke 23.34); they are a sign of his power and authority (see also Luke 5.21, 24). Too often in the history of the Church, a misunderstanding of the nature of forgiveness has led to the further disempowerment of the already powerless. Christians may at times be called to endure great trials (1 Peter 2.20), but this is not the same as colluding with personal or systemic abuse through denial or self-blame. People who have been abused may indeed be able to forgive, but this is essentially something that happens after the abuse has ceased and there has been some natural redress of the power imbalance.

Forgiveness is thus paradoxically associated with power and strength rather than with weakness. Because true forgiveness involves accepting the fact of an assault on one's identity by another person, it is deeply painful. The assault is engaged with instead of denied, so that it can become incorporated into one's sense of identity, and not be allowed to destroy it. We see this process supremely in the death and resurrection of Jesus. He carries his wounds – the stigmata of the cross – in his victorious resurrection body (Luke 24.39, 40).

The human forgiveness we have been describing is essentially a healthy, though rare and costly, life-enhancing response. There is emerging evidence for its positive effects on health and well-being.[10] Psychological understandings of forgiveness identify three components:

1 Recognizing that you have been wronged (and therefore having a sense of who you are and what is due to you).
2 A voluntary decision to respond with mercy and not to enforce 'justifiable retribution and retaliation'.
3 An outcome intended to establish, restore or promote good relations.

(after Enright and Coyle)[11]

The father in this story clearly conforms to 2 and 3, but nothing is said about 1. It is the invisible parts of the process – so invisible that it may look as if the father doesn't recognize that any wrong has been done or have any idea that he is in some sense entitled to retribution. This is perhaps why the older son sees fit to remind him of just how bad the behaviour of 'this son of yours' has been. He is wondering – speaking in contemporary psychological terms – if his father is in denial. In the same way, Jesus' glad welcome of the 'sinners' seems to have given the impression that he was unaware that their behaviour and lifestyle raised any issues at all. This is most clearly seen in the incident of the woman who washed Jesus' feet. A Pharisee reflects, '. . . If this man were a prophet, *he would have known* what sort of woman it is who is touching him – that she is a sinner' (Luke 7.39). Jesus responds to this accusation by talking about *forgiveness* of sins, also using the image of debt cancellation, making it very clear that he is well aware of this woman's history. His forgiveness is not based on naivety or denial: it is authentic.

Human forgiveness is an analogy for the forgiveness of God. There are of course limits to applying a human understanding of forgiveness, debt cancellation and the like to the forgiveness of God. Nevertheless there is a close connection between the two. Again and again in the Gospels Jesus makes the point that our forgiveness of each other flows from and is made possible by the fact that we have been forgiven. The forgiveness of others is a natural response to our encounter with the forgiveness of God, and as we forgive others we are acting like God (see for example Matthew 18.21–35; Luke 7.36–50; 6.37; 17.3–4, and a related point: 1 John 4.19, 20).

Forgiveness and release are marks of the day of the Lord's favour, a sign of the presence of God's kingdom. We can forgive unconditionally because we have been touched by, or participated in, the coming in of the kingdom of God. As Zacchaeus is honoured by Jesus' visit to his home (and thus experiences the kingdom) his natural response is to cancel illegal debts and to contribute to the release of the poor from their financial burdens.

Luke's version of the Lord's prayer is very simple:

Father, may your name be revered;
Your kingdom come.
Give us each day our daily bread.
And forgive us our sins, for we forgive everyone indebted to us.
And do not bring us to testing.   (*Luke 11.2–4*)

Because of this simplicity we can see clearly the connection between the fatherhood of God, the coming in of his kingdom, the satisfaction of our hunger by the gift of bread and the forgiveness or cancellation of sins and debts. The prodigal son returns home because he hopes for bread, but he also receives forgiveness and reconciliation with his father.

The forgiveness that the coming of God's kingdom brings is a communal affair in which we are caught up. God forgives us and we forgive each other. So in this story it is not enough for the father that his younger son has returned home: the forgiveness must touch his relationship with his older son and the relationship between the older son and his brother. The theme of encounter applies to both sons in this story. First the father goes out to meet his younger son; later he goes out to meet his elder son, and pleads with him to join the party. In response the son distances himself from both his father and 'this son of yours'. It is as if the father has really been diminished in his eyes; his love is not worth having. The father counters with 'this brother of yours' – a reminder that they are all in the same family – that, as it were, 'he too is a son of Abraham', and addresses his older son as 'child'. This is intimate familial language, perhaps expressing affection, perhaps a response to the childish attitude taken by the young man, perhaps indicating frank disapprobation.

So, the story does not end 'happily ever after' at all. We are left in ignorance of the final response of the older son. Perhaps he goes in and joins the feast, is reconciled with his brother, forgives himself for having chosen a strategy that did not altogether deliver as he had expected. Perhaps he turns and walks away, ignoring the pleading of his father. If he does this he has judged himself through judging his brother (Romans 2.1) and refusing to participate in his father's forgiveness. We start to see that the good news of the Son of Man who comes to seek out and save the lost can be bad news for some.

8

Praiseworthy pragmatism

He said (to his disciples as well): 'There was a rich man who had a manager who was denounced to him for squandering his possessions. So he summoned him and said to him, "What is this that I hear about you? Hand over your management records, for you cannot be my manager any longer." The manager said to himself, "What am I going to do now, as my master is taking the management away from me? I don't have the strength to dig, and I'm ashamed to beg. I know what I will do so that when I have been dismissed as manager people will welcome me into their homes." So, summoning each one of his master's creditors he said to the first, "How much do you owe my master?" He replied, "A hundred drums of olive oil." He said to him, "Take your contract, quickly sit down and make it fifty." Then he said to another man, "How much do you owe?" He replied, "A hundred bags of wheat." He told him, "Take your contract, and make it eighty." And the master praised the dishonest manager because he had acted sensibly; for the worldly are more sensible than the godly in responding to their moment in history. I tell you, use your dishonest wealth to make friends for yourselves, so that when it is gone, you will be welcomed into eternal homes.' *(Luke 16.1–9)*

'The master praised the dishonest manager.' Few words in the New Testament have caused more controversy or confusion. For we know (or so we think) that Jesus cannot really have told a story in which a dishonest man is praised. And so this parable, perhaps more than any other in the Gospels, is subject to much 'interpretation' and debate: what does it mean if we know that it can't mean what it seems to say?

Professional interpretation can be brought into play to mitigate the potential offensiveness of the parable. The particular challenges it poses mean that the process can become quite contrived – a massaging of the message so that it becomes appropriate on the lips of a religious teacher. Nevertheless the path taken by many commentators is to attempt to 'make sense' of the parable by making it 'sensible'. Thus we can find detailed explanations of how the manager's actions were in fact to the master's benefit: for example, that the reduction of the loans will have given the master a glorious reputation for generosity.[1] Other interpretations suggest that the manager was being virtuous by righting his master's wrongs: for example, that he was removing illegal interest from loans which his master had made.[2] Both of these approaches are at their heart ways of turning the protagonist from 'dishonest manager' into 'virtuous-if-a-little-crafty' manager, a move that is reflected in English Bibles. These tend to translate *fronimos/fronimoteroi* (translated above as 'sensibly'/'more sensible') by loaded words such as 'shrewd' or 'cunning', when it is a straightforward word meaning 'sensible, thoughtful, prudent, or wise'.

Such interpretations, however, only succeed by disregarding the actual words of the parable. The story begins by making clear that the manager had been *squandering* his master's possessions. This is a story about a manager who has been siphoning off money which wasn't his, and spending it on himself. He is not an ancient Robin Hood stealing from the rich to give to the poor; the proceeds of the manger's activities are probably simply fuelling his own lifestyle. It is worth noting that the word translated here as 'squandering' is the same word (and a relatively rare one) used in 15.13 to describe the younger son spending his inheritance in riotous living.

Then, when the manager is sacked by his master, his only thoughts are of self-preservation – there is no sign of an attack of conscience, even if one could speculate that these debts were the result of loans contravening some interpretations of the Jewish law against charging interest (Exodus 22.25). Furthermore, the amounts involved are large (about 20 times the annual rent from an individual family's plot of land) and the creditors are depicted as being literate – hardly the marks of the exploited poor. The manager then deceives the creditors into thinking that he is still in the rich man's employ: exploiting the fact that he is still in possession of the contracts, he asks, 'How much do you owe my master?' not 'my former master'. This culminates with the final sentence in which the manager is unambiguously labelled 'dishonest' (indeed in most contexts the word used, *adikia*, would simply be translated as 'wicked'). In contrast, there is no hint of a criticism of the master.

Again, this parable is firmly separated off by many commentators from those which precede it. They would argue that the three parables in Chapter 15 are about salvation for the lost and are worthy of Jesus. The parable of the dishonest manager is different, awkward, and best kept in isolation. It is an oddity which has been preserved, and because it has no clear meaning it cannot fit into a context. Thus the best one might say is that the mention of money is taken up in the pronouncement which follows, and the parable of the rich man and Lazarus at the end of Chapter 16. This isolation of the parable itself influences the interpretative strategies applied to it, for if it is separated from any context its meaning can be open to a broader range of interpretations.

This sort of approach is also as unnecessary as it is mistaken for, as we discussed in Chapter 3, the purpose of parables is to challenge. They are designed precisely not to conform to our ideas of how things ought to be, but rather to present us with disturbing ideas whose purpose is to force us to reconsider how things actually are. If we allow the parable to cause us discomfort we give it the respect it deserves.

Where does this leave us? It leaves us with exactly what we should expect, if we have learnt anything from the previous parables. We are left with a disturbing story, which culminates with the wrong ending: a good shepherd wouldn't abandon the sheep; sinners are not like blameless coins; the father shouldn't have acquiesced to his younger son's request for money nor run to welcome him back; the elder son has justice on his side; the dishonest manager shouldn't be praised. Of course, all this fits the context well for, as we have seen, Jesus is telling these parables to explain his shocking behaviour of welcoming the wrong kinds of people. The ending of the parable, with its depiction of two groups – the worldly and the godly (literally 'the sons of this age' and 'the sons of light') – points us directly back to the context established in 15.1–2 of 'the tax collectors and sinners' and 'The Pharisees and the scribes'. In a sense this parable continues the development we have seen in this sequence of parables, as each is more shocking than the previous. This is the last straw. In it Jesus pushes the boundary from shock to outrage, and from the defence to the attack. In the parables of the lost, Jesus defended 'the sinner who repented' but passed no comment on the 'ninety-nine righteous people who do not need to repent'. The story of the elder brother challenged envy and a lack of acceptance and is darker in tone, introducing the notion of self-exclusion and thus alluding to judge-ment. But now criticism is unambiguously focused on 'the godly', presumably 'the Pharisees and the scribes'. They need to consider their own position. (Interestingly, the parable is explicitly said to be told 'to his disciples as well' – are they in danger of defining themselves as the new 'sons of light'?)

The rightness of accepting that the parable really does praise and, in some way, encourage emulation of the dishonest manager is further supported by the observation that there are other occasions in Luke's Gospel in which 'bad characters' are used to make a good point.[3] The parable of the persistent widow and the unjust judge (Luke 18.1–8), the parable of the friend woken in the night (Luke 11.5–10) and the teaching about 'evil' fathers who give their own children food (Luke 11.11–13) all make the same point: do not be afraid to be bold and persistent in prayer. Boldness and persistence work even in this fallen world – learn from it and apply it in your approach to the kingdom of God. These examples show that Jesus was firmly in touch with the way the world is, with the reality of human nature, and was quite prepared to be pragmatic in his use of recognizable human behaviour to illustrate a point, even if we would not label this behaviour as good. We will return to this idea of pragmatism later in the chapter as we consider whether Jesus is not just pragmatic in his use of examples, but actually praises pragmatism itself.

Despite all the heat it generates, the parable of the dishonest manager is basically straightforward. It is the story of a wicked man, whose crimes catch up with him: the manager is sacked. In real life, of course, a sensible employer would not allow a time gap between telling the manager he is sacked, and getting him to hand over all the records and contracts. In modern parlance he would be 'escorted off the premises', precisely to avoid this kind of fraud. But surprisingly (and we will return to this) there is a 'window of opportunity', a brief moment in which the manager knows what is about to happen, but it has not yet happened. Notice that he does not try to protest his innocence, or provide excuses: he knows that he is guilty and that there is nothing he can do to get his job back. He recognizes the situation he is in and looks to the future, assessing what options are open to him. He then acts; decisively. He only has a moment: the window of opportunity is fleeting. The haste is emphasized by his telling the first creditor to 'quickly sit down', and the brevity of the conversation with the second. Any minute the master or some of the other servants might realize what is going on, or news might leak that he is the manager no more. His action is then praised. One can argue whether it is 'the master' who praises him, or 'the Lord' referring to Jesus (for Greek uses the same word, *kurios*, for both) but it matters little: his action is praised. The explanation is then given, contrasting the way in which 'the godly' and 'the worldly' react to 'their moment in history'. The manager might be dishonest, he may be far from godly, but when crisis came he reacted decisively. His wealth might have been 'dishonest', but when he realized that it was about to disappear he traded it for a more permanent benefit. For that he is praised, and held up as an example.

This parable is in continuity with those that precede it. The three parables in Chapter 15 are about the lost finding salvation; so too is this parable. The dishonest manager fits into the same category as the sheep, the coin and the prodigal son – all four are in some sense lost, all four end up in safety finding their 'homes'. Of course, there are many differences. In particular, as we will explore further below, there are differences of perspective and of timing. Nevertheless, the parable is part of a developing sequence.

The moment of crisis

Throughout Jesus' ministry there is a strong sense that now is the critical moment. This is present in all of the Gospels: for example, in John's Gospel it is expressed through the charting of the approach of 'the hour' from being 'not yet' to 'coming' to 'having come' within the first 12 chapters (for example, John 2.4; 4.21; 12.23). In Mark's Gospel Jesus' first words are: 'The time has been fulfilled, and the kingdom of God is near, repent, and believe the good news' (Mark 1.15). These words are almost paradoxical: one might imagine that if the time has been fulfilled, then the kingdom would have arrived, but no. The kingdom is only near, very close, and now is the time to react; in Mark's language, a chance to 'repent and believe'. In the next chapter we will consider more generally what the phrase 'kingdom of God' might mean, and how Luke presents the idea of a 'window of opportunity'. For now, though, we simply need to notice that this is exactly what the dishonest manager has.

As we observed earlier, the surprising feature of the parable is that the manager has the opportunity to rewrite the contracts after he has been told that he will no longer be the manager. This would not be standard procedure, for the obvious reasons which the parable makes clear! Thus the parable goes beyond the simple story of a manager who is sacked, just as in the previous parables the shepherd and the father did not act as would be normal in real life. The details of the parable have been shaped by the point Jesus is trying to make. He is telling a story in which the dishonest manager is given an unexpected stroke of fortune: the chance to do something, after being told that he is being removed but before this actually happens. In the language of Jesus' words in Mark, his dismissal 'has been fulfilled' and his expulsion 'is near' (but has not actually happened yet), therefore he should seize the opportunity. This *opportunity* is the *good news*. Within the context of Jesus' ministry the implication is that contrary to expectations (hence the Pharisees' confusion and indignation) there is a second chance for people. But what will the dishonest manager do with this opportunity? What will he do in the moment of crisis?

The manager recognizes his situation. Like the lost son, when the moment comes he appraises the situation accurately. In this story the option appraisal is explicit – 'I don't have the strength to dig, and I'm ashamed to beg.' For the lost son there is a gradual slide and awakening of a sense that there must be a better way; for the manager the disaster appears suddenly. But both men are brutally honest with themselves, see a chance of a way out, and take it. There is action.

The praise of the manager, on its own, could seem confusing or at least ambiguous – in what way is his action praiseworthy? However, the final sentence – the 'punchline' – makes the reason clear, 'for the worldly are far more sensible than the godly in responding to their moment in history'. The word *genea*, translated here as 'their moment in history', is literally 'their generation' and thus is often mistakenly translated as 'their kind'. Understood in this way, the message becomes that the worldly are better at dealing with the worldly ('their kind') than are the 'godly'. Godly people need to be more shrewd, and should not get taken for a ride; a rather bland message, which makes little sense in the context. However, the other uses of the word *genea* in Luke's Gospel make clear that there is an alternative interpretation that fits better. The word repeatedly occurs in the context of Jesus complaining about the lack of response he is receiving during his ministry. This generation is the one generation which has the opportunity of a direct meeting with Jesus, and yet it is failing to seize the opportunity (Luke 7.31; 9.41; 11.29–32; 17.25); it is the crucial generation in history (Luke 11.49–51; 21.32). Therefore in this passage 'their generation' means the point of history where the hearers find themselves face to face with Jesus.

The parable is thus about how one responds to the moment – of crisis, of decision and of opportunity – which Jesus brings. The dishonest manager, when faced with disaster, but given a final moment before judgement falls, acts decisively. Thus again we see the coherence with the previous three parables, all of which are told by Jesus to defend and explain the response of the tax collectors and sinners to his ministry. The same is true of this parable.

It is not about money, but about *response to the moment of opportunity which comes in Jesus.*

The manager, like the tax collectors and sinners, may be wicked, but at least he has the wisdom to abandon all self-delusion and hopes that 'it might just work out', is honest as to his true situation, and does something about it. The 'worldly' respond to the situation, the moment of history, in which they find themselves. In comparison, the scribes and Pharisees (the 'godly') are listening, engaging, debating and complaining about Jesus, but they are not making a decision, and soon it will be too late. If Zacchaeus had been one of them, he would still have been up the tree considering carefully the right course of action long after Jesus had travelled on from Jericho. This parable makes sense, and fits its context well, once we realize that it is not about how one should handle wealth, but how one should handle 'the times'; it does not present a morality for an ongoing life, but a picture of responsiveness to the moment of crisis.

Pragmatism

Spirituality and pragmatism are often seen as diametric opposites: being spiritual is thought to be unworldly, focused on 'higher things', idealistic; while to be pragmatic is thought to be hard-nosed, down-to-earth, and pursuing narrow self-interest. But in this story it is the manager's pragmatism that is praised. This is one of the features that makes the parable disturbing.

It is more comfortable to read about someone like Zacchaeus. He too reacted to the situation in which he found himself, seizing the 'window of opportunity', but he did this through expressing a desire to see Jesus, and then he repented of his extortion, committing himself to a new life. A wicked man 'finding religion' always generates a certain amount of suspicion and cynicism, but most people are happy to reserve judgement. It is a 'good thing', even if a little naive, for religious leaders to try to convert the wicked. If the wicked then live a changed life, over time we will probably accept that they have changed.

The story of the prodigal son presents a more troubling picture because, as we saw in Chapter 5, we are told something of his thought processes and they can be interpreted as both pragmatic and self-interested. Indeed, the sequence of his thoughts is (1) the hired workers in my father's house have plenty, (2) I am on the edge of starvation, and therefore (3) I will go home and say that I am sorry. Is the apology simply a device to obtain the food? Nevertheless, the prodigal son does express repentance, both in his own thoughts and to his father, so it is possible for us to ignore our slight qualms about his motives, and to read the parable 'spiritually' as the story of a sinner being convicted of his sin, repenting, and receiving salvation. The story of the dishonest manager gives us no such flexibility. In the last of these four parables, Jesus praises a man who acts pragmatically solely out of self-interest.

Our distrust of self-interested religion runs deep: making money from religion is seen as synonymous with being a fraud. We believe that 'conversion' or a strong renewal or change of belief should be the result of an 'inner conviction' – it should be a matter of the soul, mysterious or mystical, outside human analysis. It should not seem like a human decision at all, it should be a response to inner compulsion, an experience of 'being found' by God in the way that the parables of the sheep and the coin might have implied. This parable, however, seems to validate human, logical, even pragmatic, decisions over faith – the sort of processes described by the Theory of Planned Behaviour that we touched on in Chapter 5. The manager assesses his options, and chooses the only one available. The final verse further emphasizes the point: 'Make friends for yourselves by means of dishonest wealth so that when it is gone they may welcome you into the eternal homes.' Even at the last moment it is still best to transfer one's treasure from earth to heaven (Luke 12.13–31). The sensible person realizes that in the end only one thing matters. It is sensible to give up everything else to achieve it; use whatever assets you have to ensure that welcome; sell everything to buy the field in which the treasure is buried (Matthew 13.44). There is nothing wrong with being sensible.

Here we see a parallel with the other teaching in Luke's Gospel where Jesus uses 'bad characters' to make a point. There, it was 'Be bold and persistent in prayer.' Here, it is 'Seize your opportunity by the means available to you.' The general point is, 'Do what has a good chance of working based on your experience of the world – you know it makes sense!'

Thus this parable presents the heart of the problem between Jesus and the Pharisees, which we explored in Chapter 2. They felt that God needed protecting against human deceitfulness and self-interest; that Jesus was allowing himself – and therefore in some sense God – to be used by the wicked, who were coming to him out of mercenary – not spiritual – motives. (In the same way the elder son may have wanted to protect his father's integrity from possible abuse by his younger brother.) Jesus could not be so naive that he was unaware that many of the people who crowded around him were 'sinners'. But perhaps he was unaware of what was driving them to draw near. Did he really think that their actions expressed purity of heart? If he understood that these people were at least in part self-serving pragmatists, or the desperate grasping at straws, then he would realize that they were unacceptable. Impure motives are a part of 'the sort of people they are' – to paraphrase Luke 7.39. Surely such motives are a barrier to inclusion in God's kingdom?

But Jesus did not seem to mind or even to be interested in what motivated people to come to him. Were the prodigal son's motives for returning pure? Was the penitent thief truly converted or just hedging his bets? Jesus' teaching does not demand selfless motivation, but rather the conjunction of righteousness with one's own best interests. Jesus' message, after all, is meant to be good news, which means, presumably, that it will be good for people. Why is it unspiritual to recognize that it would be good for you, and choose it?

When we think about religion, we often focus on motives: *why* someone does or says something rather than *what* they do. This can allow us to justify wrong actions by pleading that our motives and intentions are good, even if our actions are not. 'I didn't mean to . . .' is an easy defence to make, though one could argue about the degree to which it changes the impact of what has been done. The other side of this coin is that good actions can be denigrated because the motivation behind them is suspect. This can form the focus of criticism and judgement by others, but it can also be a preoccupation of the person who performs the good action. The tendency to be suspicious of one's own motives is a phenomenon that has been influenced and nourished by the eighteenth-century Age of Enlightenment's distrust of all that is not rational, and by twentieth-century psychological theories that have placed a great emphasis on unconscious desires.[4] It is possible for people to feel condemned, guilty or paralysed because they know or suspect that their motives are not 'pure' or disinterested. In fact the Holy Grail of pure and disinterested motivation is almost certainly unattainable. In general the mixed bag of agendas that underlie our decisions are relatively benign and, as discussed in Chapter 5, largely accessible to conscious processing.

Thus we see in the parable of the dishonest manager pragmatism honoured and valued. It is not presented as unspiritual, and it does not need to be examined and unpicked to identify 'what is really going on'. In keeping with the gospels generally, Jesus seems to say that God is content to take people as they come. His honour does not require him to be protected from being 'taken for a ride', let down, or used. The self-interest of human beings is not necessarily a barrier to a meeting with the divine.

Different perspectives

This last parable of the sequence of four belongs with the other three. It is part of the same agenda, part of Jesus' defence of his own actions in welcoming the tax collectors and sinners. However, it presents a different perspective on the question of how humans meet with God.

The parables of the lost sheep and the lost coin depict a God who is active in searching for the lost. The parable of the lost coin in particular emphasized that one should not see this finding as being merely for human benefit. It was the woman who was overjoyed, not the coin (just as it was Mary rather than the teenage

Jesus who was overcome with emotion when they were reunited in the Temple). God himself wants to find the lost.

The story of the lost son introduces the human point of view, the point of view of the lost. It is the supreme parable about human meeting with God. It is not surprising that throughout history it has been the fount of much Christian spirituality, and at the heart of many people's journey to God. It captures in a single story both the human perspective and the divine. We empathize with the lost son, as he seeks independence only to find that it leads to humiliating slavery and the degradation of his very humanity. As he then latches on to a glimmer of hope that, however badly he has wronged his father, there would still be a welcome and a life better than this, we too are given hope. We feel for the father, allowing himself to be hurt by his son, waiting patiently for him to change his heart, and then being overjoyed to welcome him back. We can even identify with the elder son, and in him see our tendency to appeal to concepts like 'justice' to explain our disquiet at God's generosity, and in him we see also the destructive nature of human envy. Nevertheless, this parable does not have it all.

The story of the dishonest manager goes further and focuses even more sharply on human thought processes, wishes and actions, on the experience of being lost, of having lost everything. It validates a pragmatic response: praising the person who, despite all he has done in the past, recognizes and seizes the moment. This parable also adds three new elements. First, as we have seen, it depicts a moment of acute crisis. This contrasts with the situation of the prodigal son. He does not experience a sudden downturn of fortunes; we are not told of a particular moment when he 'comes to himself'. Instead his situation gradually gets worse, its onset is insidious, and he slides into a state of chronic unhappiness. It takes some time for it to dawn on him that there is a better way.

Second, the dishonest manager takes a leap in the dark. He does not know whether his scheme of gaining favour with the creditors will work. He puts his faith, in effect, in the sense of obligation which he hopes the creditors will feel towards him in the future and, perhaps, in the master not wanting to risk the loss of face which trying to reinstate the full debts would cause. He has no real reason to have confidence that the future will work out as he hopes, and it is unlikely that he could be a perpetual guest going from one grateful creditor to another; but he has nothing to lose. He might as well try it. The prodigal son is somewhat different. It is true that he does not know how he will be received when he returns. However, his decision is based on the fact that he remembers his father's house. He remembers that his father's hired men did not starve and had some dignity. He acts on the basis of knowledge.

Third, the parable of the dishonest manager does not really appeal to our emotions. It does not tell of the separation distress of parent and child, human and animal, the joy of reunion, the sense of hurt when one feels rejected. It does not take place in the context of an existing love relationship. It is entirely unsentimental. The account is of course full of implicit emotion – the fear of destitution which concentrates the manager's mind on finding a solution. But his response is calculated and essentially focused on his own survival, not the rebuilding of a relationship. Nevertheless, his pragmatic good sense and decisiveness is praised and held out as an example to the 'godly'. From the human perspective, the meeting with God does not need to be laden with emotional baggage.

This sense of different perspectives and new elements is important. This is partly because the same event can always be seen from different perspectives. After all, what is being described is a two-way meeting. One could say that at one and the same time, God is searching for the individual and the individual is making a decision to turn to God. The meeting can be good news for the individual, and can bring joy to God.

However, it also warns us to resist the pressure to construct a prescriptive psychology of the human–divine meeting, as if there is a set pattern which it must follow. By being presented with this set of four parables on the same topic, we are encouraged to see that this meeting can be experienced in different ways. The way it felt for us is not the way it must feel for others. The different parables will resonate with the distinctive experiences of different people. Some do tell of their initial meeting with Jesus as an experience of 'being found', or indeed of God 'chasing after them', a divine searching from which they could not escape. For others it starts as a leap in the dark at a moment of crisis, and ends with a feeling of being caught. Some feel this as a 'coming home', turning round and finding God waiting there for them, others that it is a new beginning. Many experience it in emotional, relational, terms. Others feel a far closer affinity to the dishonest manager, and may be relieved to find that a more matter-of-fact approach is valid too. (This is a particularly important point to bear in mind in the case of people who have difficulty in processing or expressing emotion, for instance people with autistic spectrum disorders. These people can indeed have an authentic relationship with God, but it may not *feel* like what we conventionally understand such a relationship to be.) What remains constant across all of these experiences is the love of God. The precise way that this is apprehended by different human beings in different situations is highly variable.

It is perhaps too easy for a church to base its pastoral and missionary approaches on a single set pattern by which it thinks that the divine–human meeting happens.[5] Indeed, the core defining identity of a church may be closely related to its understanding of how this meeting occurs. This understanding may unwittingly be dominated by characteristics that turn out to be psychological rather than theological (a high degree of emotion, a sense of guilt, a sudden decision, a particular type of 'sense of presence'). A church may gather to itself, and promote as role models, those who conform to a particular pattern. Yet these four parables together show that there is no single way in which this meeting can be adequately described. In presenting such a psychologically diverse group of protagonists and situations they affirm that the psychology of being lost, and found by God, is equally diverse.

A message for the Pharisees

'Whoever can be trusted with very little, can be trusted with much, whoever is dishonest with very little, is also dishonest with much. Therefore, if you have not been trustworthy with dishonest wealth, who will trust you with true riches? If you have not been faithful with someone else's property, who will give you your own? Nobody can serve two masters. For either he will hate one and love the other, or be devoted to one and despise the other. You cannot serve both God and wealth.' When they heard all this, the Pharisees ridiculed him, because they loved money. He told them, 'You strive to make other people think well of you, but God knows your hearts. What is most praised among people is hated by God.'

(Luke 16.10–15)

These sayings bring us to the end of this sequence of parables. With their mention of the Pharisees 'hearing all this' they link back to 15.1–2, and remind us of their context. Jesus has not given this teaching in a vacuum: it is his response to the grumbling about his welcome of tax collectors and sinners. The first paragraph (verses 10–12) forms a bridge from the parables to Jesus' direct attack on the Pharisees in verses 13–15, drawing out one further nuance from the parable of the dishonest manager.

This story praises a man's single-minded commitment to a cause – in his case the cause of self-interest. Whoever you serve, you must do it single-mindedly. It praises his insight in appraising his situation as dire, not deluding himself, and acting effectively to remedy it. It indirectly praises those who are jumping aboard the Jesus bandwagon no matter what their motives. But it also seems to contain a message that is specifically directed at the Pharisees.

Any Jewish parable concerning a rich man, king or landowner and his managers, servants or tenants is likely to be a parable about God and his people. In the gospels the basic identification is used many times: the wheat and the tares (Matthew 13.24–30), the unmerciful servant (Matthew 18.23–5), the labourers in the vineyard (Matthew 20.1–16), the tenants in the vineyard (Matthew 21.33–46; Mark 12.1–12; Luke 20.9–19), the great feast (Matthew 22.1–14; Luke 14.16–24), the steward (Matthew 24.45–51; Luke 12.42–6), the wise and foolish girls (Matthew 25.1–13), the talents (Matthew 25.14–30; Luke 19.11–27) and the watchman (Mark 13.34–5; Luke 12.35–8). Therefore when we read this parable, we should consider what sense it would have if we understand the dishonest manager to be a representation of the Pharisees. For just as the manager had been appointed by the rich

111

man to look after his affairs, so too the Pharisees (and in general the religious leadership) had been appointed by God.

The parable would then contain a direct criticism of the Pharisees, accusing them of squandering God's resources, using their position for their own benefit (see Luke 11.37ff.). If the link via the word 'squandering' to the lost son is noticed, then the criticism becomes more offensive. For the lost son abandoned his people, joined himself to the foreigners, consorted with prostitutes, and ended up feeding the unclean pigs. He did everything to which the Pharisees were opposed. Furthermore the parable begins at the point that the rich man has decided to remove the management from the dishonest manager. Does this imply that God has decided to remove the Pharisees and other religious leaders from their place as the managers and guides of his people?

In the parable, the manager acts decisively and summons those who are indebted to the rich man, and offers release from those debts. Should the Pharisees be responding to the situation they find themselves in, rather than muttering about Jesus' actions? Indeed, should they be following his actions and offering forgiveness and release to those indebted to God?

In this context verses 10–12 take on a clearer meaning. The Pharisees have been entrusted with God's property, and yet they have not been found faithful. This criticism of them is made elsewhere (Luke 11.37–54). They have betrayed the trust given them, and now at the final moment, they are stuck in self-delusion, grumbling at what Jesus is doing. At least the dishonest manager realized the game was up. In Chapter 7 we saw that the older son is unwilling to join the party despite his father's pleadings because he thinks that the party is not worth attending if his brother is there. He also feels that the fact that a party has been thrown for his brother implies that he is worth less to his father, and this makes him angry and indignant. What he does not do is to understand fully the implication of his own words, 'I have been working like a slave for you . . .'. He too has been in a bad situation for some time. In a sense, he too has somehow got lost even while being the good boy who stays home on the farm. He needs to join the party for his own sake, and indeed has been invited so to do.

Yet, unlike his brother and the dishonest manager, he cannot admit this to himself, and instead attempts to occupy the moral high ground by denigrating his father, his brother and the party.

We return explicitly to the dispute between the Pharisees and Jesus in the second paragraph (16.13–15). In the parables Jesus has responded to their grumbles about his welcome of the tax collectors and sinners. Now he turns the tables and makes his own accusation against them, seeming to summarize all that he has said in the slogan, 'You cannot serve both God and wealth' (the word for wealth here – *mamôn* – encompasses all forms of possessions or worldly status).

In theory the Pharisees should have agreed. So why did they laugh? First, like the elder son, they lacked insight, thinking that they were serving God rather than worldly things. Second, they thought Jesus was contradicting himself, for how can you claim to serve God and yet welcome sinners unconditionally? The only other time we are told that people laugh at Jesus is as he hangs on the cross, when the self-contradictory nature of his mission seems clear: 'He saved others; let him save himself if he is God's chosen Messiah' (Luke 23.35).

Jesus does not let this pass. He speaks out directly against the Pharisees. It is they, the Pharisees, who love money; who serve wealth not God. They say that they are promoting devotion to God, but in fact they are concerned more about earthly things – what people think of them. They are serving being praised by the people, rather than serving God. Is this blanket accusation fair? To take it as a literal description of all Pharisees would be a mistake.[6] But when we look back at the opening verses of our chapters, the point becomes clear. The Pharisees' complaint is that Jesus was publicly accepting the wicked. In the parables Jesus proclaims that he is simply doing what God is doing – seeking out and welcoming the lost: doing ridiculous things such as a shepherd abandoning his ninety-nine sheep on the hillside, the father rushing out to meet and honour the son who wished him dead, the rich man praising the manager who had swindled him.

These things do look foolish, as did Jesus' welcome and acceptance of the sinners. Jesus' claim, though, was that by doing these

113

things he was acting exactly as God would act. He was serving God; while the Pharisees had become complacent and obsessed by their reputation, how they would look, what people would think, how standards should be maintained. Starting with the best of intentions, and more than a grain of truth, they had somehow lost the plot. They would have hated to be thought of as serving wealth, or seeking human praise, but Jesus' ironic accusation was that this was in fact what they were doing. (Paul – a Pharisee himself – says some very similar things about well-motivated zeal for God's law going horribly wrong, in Romans Chapters 2 and 10.) Zacchaeus might have been rich, but he was determined to see Jesus despite the opposition of the crowds around him, and when given the opportunity to be devoted to Jesus, he readily gave up his wealth. Jesus is asking whether the Pharisees are prepared to give up their dependence on the good opinion of others and their habitual religious ways of thinking, and to participate in the opportunity for release and freedom that he offers. Perhaps there is a message here for us too.

9

The window of opportunity

————◆◆◆————

Until John it was the law and the prophets; since then the good news of the kingdom of God is being proclaimed and all are forcing their way in. It is easier for heaven and earth to pass away than for the tiniest part to fall from the law.   (*Luke 16.16–17*)

Something new

'Until John . . . since then': this expresses in a nutshell the cause of both the joy and the grumbling at Jesus' ministry. Jesus was doing something new, and inevitably the new challenges those who benefit from the current context and are 'at the top', and is supported by those 'at the bottom'. The announcement of the coming of God's kingdom is the announcement of a revolution: the good news of the kingdom in comparison, or even in contrast, to the law and the prophets. The Greek has the nuance: 'the kingdom of God is being proclaimed *as good news*'. But, while the coming of God's kingdom would traditionally have been presented as good news (for example, Isaiah 52.7), it is not so clear that its arrival would actually have been welcomed by all.

The phrase 'the kingdom of God' is one which is familiar but largely opaque to many Christians; we believe that it is a good thing, associate it with the teaching of Jesus, and yet would baulk if someone asked us to define it. However, what matters for understanding this paragraph in Luke's Gospel is not so much what Christianity has come to understand by 'the kingdom of God' as what Jesus' first hearers would have made of it. Here, fortunately, we are on somewhat firmer ground. The kingdom of God would have been seen as meaning *God* – as opposed to other rulers – being king, and thus in general the overthrow of existing political and social systems and their replacement by structures willed by God. Jesus' contemporaries differed in how they thought that this would occur, and the nature of any human representatives through whom God would have ruled (for example, a king like David, or perhaps through the Temple),[1] but the basic meaning is clear. It is notable that one of the slogans of the Jewish revolt against Roman rule, which came about 40 years after the death of Jesus, was 'no king but God!'[2] Nobody would have thought that the coming of God's kingdom would be a solely 'spiritual' event.

Now, if the kingdom is understood to be a theocratic state it is bad news for those who have not complied with or are excluded by the religious laws. Imagine that people start proclaiming that the United Kingdom is going to become 'God's Kingdom'. Many of us would be worried. For we would fear that 'God's Kingdom' might mean something like the regime in modern-day Iran – a kingdom run by people who claim to speak for God. This gives us a good insight into the feelings which the arrival of the 'kingdom of God' might have produced in some of Jesus' hearers, particularly the 'tax collectors and sinners'. While it may have had some connotations of things changing for the better, their concern would have been that it would mean power and rule by the very religious leaders and teachers who had excluded, shamed and condemned them.

The coming of God's kingdom is also traditionally associated with judgement – good news if you believe that you are righteous, but bad news if you feel that you do not measure up. This would be especially bad news for people who consorted with gentiles, for it was understood that God's judgement was primarily directed against other nations (see for instance Zechariah 12—14; Daniel 2 and 7).

But, says Jesus, the kingdom is good news *for everyone*. So instead of the coming of God's kingdom being bad news for people like the 'tax collectors and sinners' who had assumed they are 'out', it starts to become an uncomfortable prospect for those who had assumed that they were 'in', such as the Pharisees. The kingdom that Jesus describes has no room for the sort of elitism from which they have benefited, but welcomes all comers. This is why it is not just announced, but proclaimed as good news.

The verb used here for proclaiming the good news is also found in Jesus' 'manifesto' speech in the Nazareth synagogue at the beginning of his ministry:

> The Spirit of the Lord is upon me, because he has anointed me to *proclaim good news* to the poor. He has sent me to announce release for the prisoners and recovery of sight for the blind, to let the oppressed go free, to proclaim the year of the Lord's favour.
>
> *(Luke 4.18–19, quoting Isaiah 61.1–2)*

Note the contrast between this and Luke's account of the preaching of John the Baptist in the previous chapter:

> You brood of vipers! Who warned you to flee from the impending wrath? Bear fruit worthy of repentance . . . The axe is already at the root of the trees; every tree therefore that does not bear good fruit is cut down and thrown into the fire.   *(Luke 3.7–9)*

It is evident that something new has happened since John. When speaking of John to the people, Jesus makes this division clear: 'I tell you, no one born of a woman is greater than John; yet the least in the kingdom of God is greater than he' (Luke 7.28). John is great, indeed the greatest of the prophets, but fundamentally he is part of an earlier or different enterprise. It is 'until John . . . since then'. Jesus had such respect for John's ministry that he was baptized by him (Luke 3.21). But that ministry was part of the old order. We get further clues to this earlier in the Gospel, when Luke first records a clash between Jesus and the Pharisees and scribes because he is eating and drinking with tax collectors and sinners. The criticism is stated: 'John's disciples frequently fast and pray, just as the disciples of the Pharisees do, but your disciples eat and drink' (Luke 5.33). Jesus answers them with a saying that refers both to his identity and to the *time*:

> You cannot make wedding-guests fast while the bridegroom is with them, can you? But the days will come when the bridegroom is taken away from them, and then in those days they will fast.
>
> *(Luke 5.34–5)*

The bridegroom's presence creates a new situation – a feast rather than fasting. But this is temporary. The wedding party will not go on for ever. There is no explicit criticism of the situation prior to the wedding, and indeed the prediction is that in the future the situation will in some ways revert to how it was before ('the days will come . . . then they will fast'). However, *now* it is different. The shepherd will soon return the sheep to the fold and get on with his work; the woman will soon put the coin away safely and get on with her work; the day after the party the household of the Running Father will return to some form of normality. But for a moment, things are different, and the celebrations are in full swing. It is good news.

The year of the Lord's favour

In Chapter 8 we saw that a strange feature of the parable of the dishonest manager is his chance, in the time between being informed of his dismissal and being required to hand over the books, to go out and rewrite his master's contracts. Without this unlikely delay by the master, he could have done nothing. In the end he was praised for his decisive action, but that action was only possible because of a 'window of opportunity'.

This idea of 'the master' giving a 'window of opportunity' is an important theme in Luke's Gospel. It is expressed particularly clearly in a parable unique to Luke:

> A man had a fig tree planted in his vineyard; and he came looking for fruit on it and he did not find any. So he said to the gardener, 'See here! For three years I have come looking for fruit on this fig tree, and still I don't find any. So chop it down! Why should it be wasting the soil?' He replied, 'Sir, let it have one more year, while I dig round it and put on some manure. If it bears fruit, so much the letter; but if not, cut it down.' (*Luke 13.6–9*)

The orchard and the vineyard are both familiar images of Israel (Isaiah 5; Jeremiah 12). The vineyard owner – God – comes to examine the fruit: is it a 'good tree bearing good fruit' (Luke 6.43)? He finds none. However, the tree is not immediately cut down; it is given a final opportunity to produce fruit. Indeed, it is *helped* to produce fruit by being cared for and fed. If after this it is still barren it will be cut down, judgement will fall on it. Judgement is not dismissed, nor is it merely postponed; rather, a window of opportunity is given, a period which is particularly conducive to growth.

Immediately after reading from the scroll of Isaiah in the Nazareth synagogue Jesus says, 'Today this scripture is fulfilled in your hearing'. This seems like an unequivocal declaration of good news. However, as we noted in Chapter 2, the proclamation contains within it a sense of limitation – '*the year* of the Lord's favour', '*today* this is fulfilled'. What of next year? What of tomorrow? Isaiah 61 heightens this sense. For Jesus has stopped his quotation in the middle of a sentence. Isaiah 61.2 reads: 'to proclaim the year of the Lord's favour, *and the day of vengeance of our God*'. If today is the year of the Lord's favour, a favourable opportunity for response, then surely the 'day of vengeance' must be coming too. Nevertheless, the quotation is curtailed on Jesus' lips. The general context is undoubtedly one of approaching judgement, but what Jesus is actually announcing is good news. For there is now a season of grace – a season of God's unexpected and undeserved generosity – before the expected judgement.

The emphasis of Jesus is thus different from that of John. For John, the chance for salvation is simply a by-product of the fact that the judgement has not come yet: judgement is approaching, but until it comes there is of course time to repent. John offers baptism as a mark of repentance. Jesus, however, announces a window of special opportunity, a significant pause rather than a mere delay, and he offers himself.

On a human level the importance of the pause is immense. For it presents the people with a chance of a fresh start. It is all too easy to challenge people to change, as indeed John does (Luke 3.10–14). But in practice, as we noted in Chapter 5 when we considered the prodigal son, the very circumstances which mean a change is required often conspire to prevent a change from taking place. This young man was able to change his behaviour because of a memory of his father which gave him a hope of something better, and a sense that he could be worth something to him, if only as a hired worker. But many people may need to have their memories stirred, or their sense of self-worth affirmed, and the possibility of hope opened up to them.

This is in effect what Jesus' travels around Galilee seeking out the lost have been about. He has been enacting the acceptance of his Father and in so doing spreading a 'rumour of hope'. God does not despise people, despite what they might have been told by the religious elite; on the contrary, he loves them and is searching for them. There is a window of opportunity now to respond, regardless of the past and of the low esteem in which they may be held by others and even by themselves. Jesus did not stand apart, exhorting the sinners to do what they were not actually capable of doing, namely repenting. (Indeed, this is exactly his criticism of the Pharisees: despite their zeal, they do not actually make it easier for the people to follow God: Luke 11.46.) He travelled round seeking out the people, welcoming the sinners, communicating God's generous love. He did not just call people to repent, but made it possible for them to turn back to God.

Nevertheless, as we have seen, Jesus' announcement of good news does seem limited to 'today', or 'the year of the Lord's favour'. He came to Jericho and passed through. The opportunity came to Zacchaeus, but it was one which he had to take there and then. The wise, like the dishonest manager, should read the signs of the times:

> He also said to the crowds, 'When you see a cloud rising in the west, you immediately say, "It is going to rain"; and so it happens. And when you see the south wind blowing, you say, "There will be scorching heat"; and it happens. You hypocrites! You know how to interpret the appearance of earth and sky, so how is it that do you don't know how to interpret the present time?'   (*Luke 12.54–6*)

Notice the repeated 'and it happens': the signs will prove to be accurate. The judgement of God, whose approach is obvious to anyone, will also happen in the end. Later in the Gospel Jesus draws on Old Testament examples to give the same message. Noah had to build the ark before it started raining. Lot had to leave Sodom before the fire and sulphur rained down. One needs to act on the signs before it is too late (Luke 17.22–37), which is of course exactly what the dishonest manager did.

We saw in Chapter 2 that much of Jesus' ministry in Luke's Gospel takes place 'on the way' to Jerusalem. He does not take a direct route, but travels throughout the villages and towns meeting with people, giving his message of the opportunity of the year of the Lord's favour. In the end, however, he arrives at Jerusalem. His reaction is revealing:

> When he drew near and saw the city *he wept over it* saying, 'If you, even you, had only recognized *on this day* the things that make for peace! But now they are hidden from your eyes. The days will come upon you, when your enemies will wall you in, encircle you, and hem you in on every side. They will crush you to the ground, you and your children within you, and they will not leave one stone on another within you; *because you did not recognize the time of your inspection.*' (*Luke 19.41–4; see also Luke 13.34–5*)

Jesus did not come to Jerusalem to bring judgement or condemnation. His arrival, its inspection, brought the opportunity for peace – peace to a city oppressed by Roman rule, peace for the people alienated from their God. (One might compare John 3.17 – 'God did not send his son into the world in order to condemn the world, but so that the world might be saved through him.') Nevertheless he is saying that Jerusalem's blindness to its need, and to the opportunity he has presented, leaves it with nothing but destruction ahead. Jerusalem has not seized the opportunity, and in some sense that window of opportunity has now closed.

Jesus weeps. That is his response as he realizes that the city will not take the proffered opportunity. It is hard to comprehend the sense of despair and frustration which must have overwhelmed him. He has spent years trying to get the people to grasp the enormity of God's love for them, that God is searching for them, that they should return to their home where they will be welcome, and yet to a great extent he has failed. The failure of Jesus' mission is a shocking idea. It may seem more acceptable to say that his mission only 'appeared to have' failed at this point. (The logic behind this is that through his death and resurrection his mission finally succeeded.) But this would be to trivialize Jesus' weeping here. Jesus' death and resurrection did not result in recognition of his identity and acceptance of his message by Jerusalem as a whole. Sadly, peace did not come to the city. Instead it was razed to the ground by the Romans 40 years later. Luke tells us that Jerusalem is supremely precious to Jesus. It has been his destination throughout all his journeys, and yet when he arrives there he is not welcomed and accepted. These are tears of bitter disappointment, hurt, frustration and loss. This is Jesus' reaction to judgement.

'The city' has not recognized the moment. (We should probably understand 'the city' – Jerusalem – as symbolic in a sense for 'the heart of the nation'. Individual people have indeed seized the opportunity, but 'the nation', particularly its religious heart, has not.) In the language of the parable of the dishonest manager, it is as if the manager has ignored both the crisis and the opportunity and has just tried to carry on as normal until the master's servants throw him out on to the street. While the manager recognized the crisis provoked by his master's inspection of his work, the city has failed to recognize even that it is being inspected. If we think back to the father's two sons, we find that the point is the same. The younger son recognizes the desperate state he is in, and takes action. The elder son is not even aware of the sense of alienation and distance between him and his father, though it soon emerges when his father welcomes his younger brother. The father then comes out to the elder son, pleading with him, but it seems that he will not respond. One can imagine the father returning to the party weeping for his now lost son, just as Jesus here weeps over Jerusalem.

Different times for different people

It would be easy to misunderstand these statements about the window of opportunity, concluding that, for example, all those in Jerusalem must have missed their chance. That this is false is made clear by what Luke writes subsequent to 19.41–4 after Jesus has already declared that Jerusalem has failed to recognize its 'inspection'. Soon afterwards, the thief on the cross asks Jesus to remember him and is told, '*Today* you will be with me in Paradise' (Luke 23.43). For that man, that moment on the cross was his moment of opportunity regardless of what was said about Jerusalem, and he, like the manager in the story, seized it wholeheartedly. Then in

Luke's sequel to his Gospel, the Acts of the Apostles, we read of many in Jerusalem responding to the message about Jesus (2.43–7; 6.7). Thus what is said about Jerusalem here, and about other places later in Acts, is about the city as a corporate entity (much as one might speak of Oxford University, Downing Street or the Church of England). The 'city' has had its chance, but this does not mean that the individuals within it, as individuals, do not also have their opportunity.

However, to focus too much on this issue of the relationship between 'the corporate' and 'the individual' is to get diverted from the point. Jesus' message is clearer and more personal. He is speaking to those listening to him on a particular occasion, saying that in his drawing near to their town or village, and in their drawing near to listen to him, they are presented with an opportunity which they should take. There is an urgency reflected in his itinerant ministry: he is always 'passing through', there for a period and then off again. Similarly, Jesus does not engage in discussion of why the people need rescue. As we have seen, parables such as the lost coin deliberately undermine discussions of blame. He simply seems to work from the point of view that people are estranged from the God who loves them – why is not important; the opportunity to return to God, to be found by him, is.

This sense of moments of opportunity is reflected in many aspects of our everyday lives. We find ourselves wondering if we should do or say something, but the moment passes and we regret a lost chance. Sometimes we will get a second chance to remember that birthday, take advantage of that special cheap offer, or summon up the courage to ask our friend on a date. But sometimes there will be no second chance. This is particularly poignant for people who have lost loved ones unexpectedly: 'If only we'd taken that holiday she wanted', 'If only I had told him how much I loved him.'

Making decisions to change direction in life also seems to be subject to an opportune moment that may all too quickly pass. Starting a diet, giving up smoking, taking up exercise, changing job and so on seem subject to a 'now or never' phenomenon. When considering change, people may move in and out of various states, described by some psychologists as 'precontemplation' – having no recognition of a need for change; 'contemplation' – awareness that there might be a problem; and 'preparation' – forming intentions. For a change of behaviour to take place the means for that change have to be available (for instance an invitation to join a self-help group), but the person also has to be in a responsive state of contemplation or preparation. The time has to be right.[3]

The same phenomenon is apparent in the way in which people do or do not respond to the Christian message. People come to a point of potentiality, a moment of readiness for decision. This may be provoked by a personal crisis or it may be a longer-term process, but readiness to respond comes to a head at some point. (Zacchaeus had heard about Jesus, had perhaps contemplated change, but then the moment to climb the tree and see him actually arrived, and when called he responded.) Some will respond to Jesus. Some, as the parable of the sower and the story of the rich young ruler tell us, will not. And those who do not respond, like the seeds, do not remain in a state of potentiality for ever. The moment passes and normal life reasserts itself. Of course, at some point in the future another similar moment may come, but that particular window of opportunity has closed. Life is not experienced just as a flat continuum, but is punctuated by moments of potential. This insight can be misused or manipulated, as in the case of the pressurized 'altar call' – proclaiming that now is the moment in which people must decide, a moment dictated by the preacher. Nevertheless, this is observed in practical Christian ministry time and time again. There is a moment of opportunity, a drawing near between a human being and God, which is either seized so that a real connection occurs, or it passes by.

Forcing their way in

The reference to 'all forcing their way in' has puzzled commentators down the centuries. It seems strange to think of people forcing their way into the kingdom of God: surely God's kingdom is a matter of peace, not violence; and you enter it by God's will, not by your own efforts? This brings us back to the difficult question of the 'meaning' of 'the kingdom of God'. We noted earlier that Jesus' hearers would have connected it with ideas such as the expulsion of their Roman oppressors, and yet its precise meaning on the lips of Jesus is not clear. The phrase occurs over 30 times in Luke, but in almost all of these it is effectively a slogan, conveying an ideal or goal whose content is not explained. It is something which is preached (for example, 9.1), it is a valuable goal or reward (as in 6.20 or 12.31), it is something which is coming, or indeed even among us (9.28 or 11.20). None of this, though, really tells us what it is. Indeed it is called a mystery (8.10) and the one time when we are given a picture to help us understand it, the picture is that of a mustard seed or yeast: small to begin with but with great consequences (13.18–19), which is useful, but doesn't answer the question of what it is. We are left with the impression that it is Jesus' way of conveying the sense of longed-for peace and justice, acceptance and welcome from both the rest of the community and from God. Many of Jesus' activities such as healing, exorcisms, celebrations and gathering the lost can be seen as aspects of the arrival of the kingdom, and yet the Gospels do not generally label them explicitly as this. Overall it is difficult to pin down the meaning of the phrase 'the kingdom of God'; like Jesus himself it remains just out of our grasp, close to us but elusive.

This need not concern us too greatly, however. For these verses are not so much about the meaning of the kingdom of God but about *entry* to the kingdom. On reflection we see that this is yet another point of connection with the four preceding parables. For they were all about the point of meeting, not what followed that meeting. We are not told about what happened to the sheep after it was rescued, nor what happened afterwards to the coin. In the parable of the lost son this is even more apparent. The father explains to his elder son that the *arrival* of his brother demanded a party. The elder son confuses this giving of a party with a statement of his worth relative to his brother. His mistake is in not understanding that the party is not so much a response to the *person* as to the *occasion*; it is about the change from 'being lost' to 'being found', the raising from 'dead' to 'alive'. This is true in general of parties – they tend to occur at what are called liminal moments, points of transition, such as an eighteenth birthday, a new job, a new house. They may appear to be about the person ('*my* birthday', '*my* new job', '*my* new house'), so the elder son's reaction is understandable. Yet a party is not an indication that the guest of honour is worth more than other people, but instead that this is a special occasion for her – her *day*. The father's pleading with his elder son effectively implies that tomorrow normal life will have to continue, and we will need to sort out how the three of us work together given the past, but today is the day of arrival, of entry, and therefore of celebration.

Yet Jesus describes a 'forced' entry. Here he is in effect repeating the point of the parable of the dishonest manager. This man was praised exactly because he forced his way in: he did anything to ensure that he would enter the 'eternal home'. 'The godly' were warned that their measured response might easily become complacency. They might never respond to God's call with the vigour and wholeheartedness which it deserves. We were warned that 'no slave can serve two masters; for a slave will either hate the one and love the other, or be devoted to the one and despise the other'. Hate and love, devotion and despising: this is what lies at the heart of one's response to God.

'Forcing their way in' points to the eagerness and energy of those who truly love and are devoted to God. Earlier Jesus told a parable to Simon the Pharisee explaining the actions of the sinful woman who had forced her way into a dinner party and washed Jesus' feet with her tears, the point of which was, 'her many sins have been forgiven; because she loved much. But the one to whom little is forgiven, loves little' (Luke 7.47). It is those who have always felt that the 'kingdom of God' meant exclusion or judgement for them who react to the good news with eagerness, love and even 'force'. 'All are forcing their way in' makes the same point, rather implying that 'the common folk' are forcing their way in – 'God's kingdom will take anyone nowadays!' Matthew's version of this phrase makes the point more starkly: 'the forceful [or even 'the violent'] are grabbing hold of it' (Matthew 11.12) and, speaking later to the religious authorities, 'Truly I tell you, the tax collectors and the prostitutes are getting into the kingdom of God ahead of you' (Matthew 21.31). The Gospels are full of references to crowds running after Jesus, pressing in to see him. Later, as Jesus approached Jericho a blind man (named as Bartimaeus by Mark) made an almighty scene calling for him (Luke 18.35–43). The crowd told him to be quiet – to be measured and respectable. But Bartimaeus was having none of it. He knew that this was his chance, and he was going to do anything he could to make sure it did not pass him by. He was going to 'force his way in', and he did.

Of course, the parables we have studied balance this sense of 'forcing one's way in' and put it in perspective by their focus on God's activity. People can only force their way in because God is at the same time searching for them. The sinners and tax collectors can only draw near to Jesus because he is travelling around the towns and villages seeking out the lost. Nevertheless, the notion of 'forcing' their way in captures the sense of the 'window of opportunity' and the need to respond. Action is necessary now; interest and debate are not sufficient. The train is pulling out of the station – the godly are discussing engineering, pricing policies and the availability of refreshments; the worldly are pushing past the ticket barriers and jumping on to the train as it starts to move. These parables do not discuss the ethics of buying train tickets, but urge their hearers to get on the train.

> People get ready
> There's a train a comin'
> You don't need no baggage you just get on board
> All you need is faith
> To hear the diesels hummin'
> Don't need no ticket you just thank the Lord[4]

The law remains

All of this talk of a new window of opportunity in which the sinners and tax collectors are welcome could suggest that the old morality and standards witnessed to in the law are now annulled. Now, after John, perhaps they are no more. This allegation is an obvious response to the message of the good news. As we discussed in Chapters 2 and 3, this is at the heart of Jesus' ongoing argument with the Pharisees and scribes, and is graphically illus-trated in the parable of the lost sheep. The Pharisees and scribes are thinking about the good of society as a whole, and the detri-mental effect on morality of Jesus' apparent message that breaking the rules and betraying one's people doesn't matter; you are welcome anyway. From their point of view, Jesus' message of God searching for the lost sheep may sound superficially attractive, but in practice it is stupid since one will lose more of the ninety-nine in the process. Something similar can be seen in the elder son's complaint to his father – your welcome of your younger son means there was no point in my following the rules, and if that is the case, why would anyone follow the rules?

In his second volume, the Acts of the Apostles, Luke depicts this as being exactly the allegation made against the Christian move-ment; it is undermining the law (Acts 6.11–14). This allegation becomes particularly focused on the welcome the Christians offered to Gentiles (Acts 15.5; 21.21). As we noted in Chapter 7, this outreach to Gentiles (the lost outside of Israel) was the natu-ral and logical extension of Jesus' own outreach to the lost within Israel, and as such it provoked the same response. The offer of welcome to sinners undermined the law, and with it morality and social cohesion. Paul in particular, as the figurehead of this move-ment to the Gentiles, appears to have had to fight constantly against this interpretation of the consequence of his message (see for instance Romans 6.1, 15; Romans 3.8; 1 Corinthians 10.23; see also James 2.14–17).

This is why 16.17 is so important as the conclusion to this section of Jesus' teaching. After all that has been said and commu-nicated in the parables about God's search for people in love, his waiting and watching, wanting to embrace the lost, and the need for people to grab hold of the opportunity at the moment in which it comes to them, the law remains.

How does this fit together? We can favour one side or the other – being attracted by the acceptance of the Running Father, or instead emphasizing the law's continuance – and carefully ignore the other. But it is no mistake that this group of parables ends on this verse: there is a genuine tension. Deeper understanding comes from wrestling with how this insistence on the law fits with the preceding parables; how the good news of the kingdom of God stands alongside the commitment that the law remains. The parable of the bridegroom quoted earlier in the chapter shows the way forward – it is true that while the bridegroom is with the guests they do not fast, but when he is gone they will. It is not that before him, one set of rules applied ('the law') and afterwards another ('welcome of the wicked'). On the contrary, it is his presence that signifies a new moment of opportunity. It is not even that while he is there, different rules apply. It is more that at that point in time, the point of meeting and celebration, other things become more important.

We see this in the story of Zacchaeus. Immediately after the meeting, while he and Jesus are still on the way to his house, Zacchaeus declares that he will change his ways (19.8), and interestingly it is only after this declaration that Jesus responds by saying that 'today salvation has come to this house' (19.9). But nevertheless, what Zacchaeus would or would not do, how he would or would not change, was not the issue at the point of meeting. That moment was solely and completely about Zacchaeus' longing, and Jesus' finding and welcoming of him.

Jesus' message produces particular difficulties for communities committed to holiness of life, whether a village in first-century Galilee or a modern-day church. For it means that at any moment most of the community will be 'on the way', living lives of discipleship, aspiring to high moral standards. However, the community also needs to be open to the fact that at any time there will be some who are at a point of entry, or perhaps re-entry, a point at which, as we have seen, moral standards and even motivation do not matter. All that matters is the person's response. These two agendas stand in tension or even conflict with each other. How does a community live as a 'holy people' (1 Peter 2.9) doing divinely ordained 'good works' (Ephesians 2.10) while simultaneously accepting the marginal or even the 'wicked'? It is a difficult tightrope to walk. A church community which itself has high moral standards can find it hard to cope with people who fall short of these standards but who wish to come in. Are we really expected to welcome the person who is involved in minor tax or social security fraud, who regularly drinks to excess, who lives in keeping with society's standards of sexual behaviour rather than those of the church – or worse? One response is to say that such standards don't matter – we need to be more 'tolerant' or to 'modernize'. Another is to keep these sort of people out – to expect them to reform before they are welcome. (This is easy to do in all sorts of subtle ways without actually showing people off the premises.) Jesus' message, expressed in this passage, is neither of these. Standards do matter – the law will remain – but these standards are not an *entry requirement*. All that is necessary for entry is the desire to turn or return to God. Transformation of life comes later.

This is a hard message to swallow, partly because upholding high moral standards is the Christian calling, partly because of the human tendency we identified in the elder brother of feeling that it's not fair if others have it too easy, and partly because the needs of a marginalized individual may seem to compromise the good of the whole. It was difficult for the Pharisees. Anyone with responsibility in the maintenance of a church community will have much sympathy with the Pharisees' logic: why risk the ninety-nine for the sake of the one – it's surely better to preserve what you have? And yet, according to Jesus, that logic runs contrary to what God is doing. God's action is paramount. Religious leaders have no place in telling God what to do. If God is searching for and accepting people, then the least the community can do is to welcome them, and with better grace than the elder brother. The best the community can do is to stop looking inward and go out searching.

In these parables Jesus answers questions about how religious people should relate to those on the margins of their community and beyond by describing what God is like. He has a heart for the lost. If we are his followers we are called to share his heart, to bring Christ to others by making it easy – not difficult – for them to seize the opportunity. If we have been forgiven, we forgive others. If we have been met where we are, we meet others where they are.

10

Meeting Jesus

That same day two of them were travelling to a village called Emmaus, which is seven miles from Jerusalem, and they were talking with each other about all that had happened. While they were talking and discussing Jesus himself drew near to them and began to travel with them, but their eyes were kept from recognising him. He asked them 'What is it that you are discussing as you are walking along?' They stopped, dejected. One of them (called Cleopas) said to him, 'Are you the only person staying in Jerusalem who doesn't know what has happened there in the last few days?' He asked them, 'What things?' and they replied, 'The things about Jesus of Nazareth, who was a man – a prophet – powerful in his actions and his words before God and all the people, and how our chief priests and leaders handed him over to be executed, and they crucified him. We had hoped that he was the one who would set Israel free. But also, alongside all this, it is now the third day since this happened, and some women from our group have now thrown us into great confusion. They were at the tomb early this morning yet were not able to find his body and returned saying that they had actually seen a vision of angels who said that he was alive. Some of us returned to the tomb and also found it just as the women had said, but they didn't see him.' He said to them, 'Oh how foolish and slow your hearts are to believe all that the prophets said. Wasn't it necessary for the anointed one to undergo these things and to enter his glory?' And beginning with Moses and the prophets he explained to them what was said about him in all the Scriptures.

When they drew near to a village to which they were going, he gave the impression that he was travelling on. They pressed him saying, 'Stay with us, because it is nearly evening and the day is already over.' So he went in to stay with them. And then, while he was eating with them, he took the bread, gave thanks and broke it and began to give it to them. Then their eyes were opened and they recognised him; and he vanished from their sight. They said to each other, 'weren't our hearts burning while he spoke to us on the road, opening the scriptures to us?'

They got up at that very moment and returned to Jerusalem and found the eleven and their companions gathered together, who were saying that the Lord had really risen and had appeared to Simon. So they explained what had happened on the road and how he had been made known to them when he had broken the bread.

(Luke 24.13–35)

The Emmaus road

In Chapter 1 we observed that meetings with Jesus do not just happen at a single point in the life of the believer – at what some would refer to as 'conversion'. Our ongoing walk of discipleship is also punctuated by repeated times of meeting with Jesus, our personal eschatological moments, which are in many ways similar to our initial meeting. In this way we are able to recognize who it is that we have met.

So, finally we turn to events on the Emmaus road. Here two people encountered Jesus, but it was not the first time these three had met. The account of this meeting can quite accurately be described as a 'resurrection appearance', a sighting of the risen Christ on the third day after his crucifixion witnessed by two disciples known to the first Christian communities in Palestine. Yet this is a very long and detailed piece of narrative, and on the way to its destination – 'the Lord has really risen' – it has much more to tell us.

The two were met, as it were, 'on the way' because they were already disciples of Jesus. (As we saw in Chapter 1, 'following the way' is Luke's expression for Christian faith.) Like the Jesus who travelled from Galilee to Jerusalem they were on a journey, travelling together in fellowship. These disciples were not part of the inner circle, the twelve. The two are ordinary, and one of them is anonymous. It is possible that Cleopas is the same character as Clopas who is mentioned in John 19.25, an uncle of Jesus by marriage.[1] We are told nothing about Cleopas' companion, and this is perhaps significant. It allows us to put ourselves in the shoes of this nameless man or woman. Thus, the account of the meeting between Jesus and these two disciples can perhaps be a model for the meeting of any Christian disciple with Jesus as we travel along the way. It can form a bridge to our own lives. Of course it is possible to draw a theological distinction between our meetings with Jesus and this meeting with the risen but not yet ascended Christ. Nevertheless, our experience is that this meeting has many resonances with our own meetings and, as we shall see, the focus on the breaking of the bread actively invites us to make such a connection.

There is something very human about these two disciples. Their reaction when Jesus asked them what they were talking about tells us much. They stopped dead, and looked dejected. The recent events had been so overpowering and traumatic for them that they could not comprehend that someone else could be ignorant of them. They were completely preoccupied: walking along the road, discussing and debating, trying to make sense of all that had happened. The problem facing them was that the story of Jesus was like the parables he told – it had the wrong ending. Along with many others, these two disciples had been convinced that Jesus was God's anointed one who would release Israel, and yet the ending – not just Jesus' death, but his conviction and sentence to a humiliating method of execution – had seemed to prove conclusively that this was mistaken. This was something that they would have been starting to absorb over the previous terrible days. Then the women's story again threatened to add a new and unsettling twist, which removed any hope of emotional closure.

In these disciples we see ourselves as we try to make sense of the world around us. What we see happening to others, or experience ourselves, frequently doesn't seem to cohere with our religious hopes. This can be true on a large scale as we hear of great natural disasters, and continuing cycles of violence, and we struggle to understand how these things can take place in God's world. On a more personal scale, our own disappointments and tragedies can seem to invalidate the idea that God is in charge of the universe, that he loves us, or that his love is worth having. In these circumstances, we often have little choice but to plod on like the two disciples, continuing on the road ruminating and preoccupied, struggling to bridge the gap between our experience and our hopes.

But for the two disciples this cycle of rumination was broken into by Jesus. The text tells us that he *drew near* (the same Greek word that we have encountered many times before) and he started to walk the way with them. So the meeting was not so much face-to-face as side-by-side. Jesus literally came alongside them, met with them, and showed them how in fact the gap between their experience and their previous hopes was not what it seemed: the Scriptures did speak of him, the events in Jerusalem had been necessary, and indeed they had been 'gloriously' necessary. Here again he brought together and held the tensions and apparent contradictions between the law and the prophets and his own ministry. In doing this he met the disciples where they were, diving right into the midst of their concerns, and in so doing helped them make sense of the world. The text makes it clear that he did not do this gently but rather spoke in tones of exasperation. And the effect on them was not merely one of intellectual resolution. There was also an emotional release – 'our hearts burning'.

Now, what is interesting about this is that the 'burning hearts' experience was used later as a piece of evidence by these two people to support their conviction that the man they had met was Jesus himself. There was something *recognizable* about it. It was an identifying mark of being with Jesus. It wasn't so much that the stranger gave an elegant exegesis of the relevant scriptural passages. It wasn't so much that he gave a good theological explanation. In fact we are told only that his answer to the question of why the anointed one had died was that 'it was necessary'. But he did make a clear connection between the Scriptures and the recent experience of the two disciples. He turned their existing ideas upside down, excited and exhilarated them, and offered them new hope, just as he had done when he spoke in parables. The 'wrong ending' of his death was shown to open up new and unthought-of possibilities.

The simplicity of the statement that 'it was necessary' also connects with the way Jesus spoke in the parables. He did not answer the 'Why?' questions, such as 'Why was the sheep lost?', 'Why wasn't there a risk-free way of finding the sheep?', 'Why did the father allow the younger son to go?', 'Why didn't he rescue his son from the foreign land?' In effect Jesus didn't answer the question, 'Why couldn't you fulfil your mission from God without offering such a shocking welcome to the tax collectors and sinners?' His answer was simply, 'This is what God is doing', with the implication that this was the only way of saving the lost whom God desperately loves. Here, on the Emmaus road, his answer to the disciples' 'Why did Jesus die?' was 'It was necessary'.

This is not a casual remark. We are told that Jesus was 'in anguish' in Gethsemane as he came to the full realization that 'it was necessary' (Luke 22.41–4). Nevertheless, this is the answer given. It is an answer which we can find unsatisfactory, but it is important to see that the disciples on the road were not given this answer alone. They also met Jesus. It is not so much that their questions were answered, but they were cast in a different light by his presence. This too is the nature of God's answer to Job. What is important to Job is not so much the answer (or non-answer) he receives to his 'Why?' questions, but rather the fact that in giving it God has met directly with him (Job 42.5). The answer to the 'Why?' question turns out to be 'Hello'.

When they came to the end of their journey, Jesus was going to travel on. Throughout most of Luke's Gospel Jesus had been traveling to Jerusalem. It had seemed to be his final destination. Now, however, we see that it was in fact only part of a greater journey. He was not going to stay with the two disciples for ever. His ministry was still itinerant, he was still passing through. The disciples responded correctly. They seized the opportunity and 'pressed him to stay'. (Interestingly the Greek word used here is closely related to the word for 'forcing' that is used to describe the entry of everyone into the kingdom of God in Luke 16.16.) Jesus would have passed on by, except for their action. They had perhaps learnt the lesson from the story of the dishonest manager.

The book of Revelation gives a very apt description of what is going on in people's meetings with Jesus. 'Listen! I stand at the door and knock. If you hear my voice and open the door, I will come in to you and eat with you' (Revelation 3.20). It certainly applies well to the case of Zacchaeus. But there is a subtle shift of emphasis on the road to Emmaus. Jesus did not invite himself to eat with the two disciples. They seized the initiative and invited him in to share a meal. They did this because having tasted the sweetness of being close to him, even without full recognition, they could not bear that it should come to an end so soon – 'Stay with us!' Nevertheless, at the end Jesus was taken from them. He could not be tied down. He was not their possession. In John's Gospel, when the risen Jesus appeared to Mary Magdalene she tried to grab hold of him, something that can be understood as a natural attachment response. But Jesus told her, 'Do not cling on to me' (John 20.17). He needed to travel on. The reunion was only temporary and the pain of separation was not over for Mary. Her experience of being with the earthly Jesus could not be relived.

Jesus accepted the invitation of the two disciples. He went in and they shared a meal. During the meal he took the bread, gave thanks, and blessed it. At last they recognized him. Why did recognition come at this point? It is likely that some familiar Jesus-characteristics had been evident to the disciples during the journey, as they later reflected. But it was during the meal, as he broke bread, that full conscious recognition happened. Throughout Jesus' ministry, as we have seen, he was known for eating and drinking, and for telling parables which culminated in a party. When Jesus broke the bread, these two people were reminded of 'their Jesus', the man whom they loved and with whom they had probably shared many meals. He was back. They could be with him again. These actions of Jesus, taking, blessing, breaking and distributing bread,[2] are described in the accounts of the feeding of the five thousand (Luke 9.16 and parallels). The feeding of the five thousand is one of the few events from the life of Jesus that is reported in all four Gospels. We must therefore understand it as definitive of Jesus in some way. The breaking of the bread came at the end of Jesus' *welcome* of the crowds who followed him, when he told them about the kingdom of God and healed the sick (Luke 9.10–11). Like the lost son, the crowds were given bread and were satisfied. The feeding of the five thousand is the great banquet, an anticipation and foretaste of the eschatological rule of God. Jesus' paradoxical and exciting teaching alerted the two disciples to his identity, they knew that it was lovely to be in his presence, but it was the sharing of the meal that was definitive.

At the last supper, while sharing a meal at Passover time, Jesus had also carried out these characteristic actions (Luke 22.19). This time he used them to allude to his coming death. The broken bread holds together the images of celebratory feasting and a suffering broken body, just as Jesus' teaching on the road held together the suffering of the anointed one with the idea of glory. By word and action Jesus reconciled these deeply contradictory notions for his disciples.

Jesus ultimately revealed himself in what is sometimes translated 'the breaking of the bread'. The connection with the Eucharist is obvious (Acts 2.42; 2.46; 20.7). The Eucharist has never been far from the heart of Christian spirituality, for spirituality is fundamentally about the human encounter with God, and Christians have found over the centuries that at the Eucharist we meet with, are embraced, and are fed by Jesus. Much ink has been used, and sadly much blood has been shed, in the debate about precisely how this happens – in attempts to localize and hold the 'presence' of Jesus. But the experience of Christians is simply that in the Eucharist 'The Lord is here!' – a Lord who is both remembered from the past and encountered in the present.

The narrative of the Emmaus road speaks powerfully to us as disciples of Jesus travelling 'on the way'. As we discussed in Chapter 1, the journey of faith is a journey from an initial meeting with Jesus to a final meeting with him, punctuated by moments or periods of re-encounter. For most people do not experience the continual, steady presence of God, but rather a cycle of ebbs and flows, moments of closeness and times of distance. For a time, Jesus came close to these disciples on the road to Emmaus, walked with them and ate with them, and then he 'travelled on'.

The effect that this meeting had on them is crucial. They were transformed from 'dejected' folk whose hopes had been dashed, who were in mourning for their leader, perhaps understandably fleeing the scene of the action of the last few days. Their meeting with Jesus left them energized and excited, having made some sense of events, and with the conviction that they had met with their Lord. Despite the lateness of the hour and the dangers of night travel, we are told that they 'immediately' got up, did a U-turn, and hurried back to Jerusalem. They wanted to tell others of their experience.

This story strikes an interesting psychological and spiritual balance. The disciples were not waiting in Jerusalem, trying to hang on to their last experience of Jesus. They were travelling on the way that seemed best to them: it was during the journey that Jesus met them. The meeting was not manufactured as a result of their efforts. Rather, it took them completely by surprise and recognition of Jesus came late in the process.[3] Nevertheless, their experience would have been incomplete had they not 'pressed him to stay'. In that sense they did need to pay attention to their need for refreshment, and to seek to make the most of the encounter. Jesus invited himself to draw near to them on the road. They invited him to stay awhile with them. It was a two-way meeting.

So, let us draw this section to a close by reflecting on the marks of our own meetings with Jesus that are not so very different in character from that meeting on the road to Emmaus two thousand years ago.

Our Lord often comes upon us unawares where we are,
He may walk the way beside us,
At first we may not recognize him,
He is as likely to bring challenge as comfort,
We see things in a new light,
What previously did not make sense starts to make some sort of
    sense, though this is often shot through with paradox,
We are nourished and refreshed,
We are energized and re-directed from our own agendas towards
    the concerns of others,
We would like the meeting to be prolonged,

The meeting may take place in the context of reading the Bible or participating in the Eucharist,

We will recognize Jesus because he will be like the Jesus we already know and the Jesus of the New Testament,

Afterwards we may have a story to tell and we will certainly have a memory to treasure,

We know that we are known and are loved,

We cannot manufacture such meetings but we can respond and invite our Lord to stay awhile,

We cannot hold on to him, but we live in hope of his return.

That is why we can say with those first Christians, '*Marana tha.* Come, Lord Jesus!'

A heart like ours?

This book has been about meeting Jesus. We began with the account of the day when Zacchaeus met Jesus. He wanted to 'see Jesus'. Jesus took this desire and brought it to fulfilment: Zacchaeus did not remain a spectator but was drawn into the centre of the action. He did not just 'see Jesus' or 'see who Jesus was' – he met him, and his life was transformed. Next we considered four parables, which taken together portray the human encounter with God – something that looks simple, but which seems to have complicated ramifications and to call up all sorts of questions.

The picture of God which is revealed to us by Jesus is disturbing. Like the shepherd and the woman, this God is driven by overpowering love for the lost, is willing to take risks for them, is not interested in attributing blame, and when he finds them experiences great joy. Like the father, he passively accepts the pain of rejection by his children, but nevertheless waits and watches and welcomes them back unconditionally with open arms. The response to the elder son and the parable of the dishonest manager show that he is not concerned about why people turn to him, nor disapproving of those scrambling to 'get on board at the last minute'. In Pauline terms he is a God who is interested in faith rather than works.

The Gospels tell of many meetings between Jesus and people. The brief yet lively and vivid interchanges between Jesus and these people hook us in psychologically. But these meetings are more than a skilful literary device. They are theologically important. The reason for this is hinted at in the way Jesus defended his welcome of the tax collectors and sinners in the parables we have studied. His practice of meeting such people was questioned, and in reply he told stories of the two-way meeting between God and human beings. We find that meeting is important, because meeting is about engagement between people, about understanding who the other truly is: his desires, concerns and attitudes. Meeting is about 'knowing' and 'being known', not 'knowing about'. The manner of Jesus' ministry, and the parables which he told about God, communicate clearly that the way we find God is through relating to him as a person who wants to find us.

This is not an obvious way to approach God, who is after all usually conceived of as transcendent. It might seem more appropriate to relate to God primarily through religious practice, philosophical enquiry, systematic theology, or ethical system. The attitude of the Pharisees exemplifies one such approach – one which emphasizes religious and ethical practice, and contrasts starkly with the approach of Jesus. We have seen that the difference between Jesus and the Pharisees was not so much about their understandings of morality, but about their understandings of God which determined how this morality was put into practice. In response to the ethical and religious questions of the Pharisees, Jesus told stories about people, and they are full of emotion. The emotion is not confined to the 'human' characters such as the lost son and his older brother, but is also there in the characters who 'represent' God. The God depicted by Jesus in these parables is essentially a person with emotions that seem very human. He seems to have a heart like ours – at any rate, a heart enough like ours to enable us to imagine what it might feel like to be God as he encounters human beings; a heart enough like ours for us to understand that this person's emotions spring from an attitude of profound love. Of course, we have seen that God's heart is far 'beyond' ours: he has a depth of compassion, a longing for the lost, and a willingness to suffer, risk and forgive which shocks us the more we understand of it. Nevertheless, we only come to understand what God is like because we are able to imagine what it might feel like to be God.

This may seem offensive, almost blasphemous – 'imagining that you are God'. Or it may be dismissed as laughable anthropomorphism. Yet it is in the tradition of the Old Testament prophets, and it is Jesus' method. But Jesus goes beyond the prophets, for his teaching is based on a uniquely intimate relationship with his Father. Thus, he is not merely sharing his opinion, his spiritual insights and visions, or what he has received from religious tradition, and using anthropomorphic language to make it accessible. He is revealing his Father's heart. In the words of the twentieth-century theologian Emil Brunner, this is not anthropomorphism – it is '*theo*morphism'.[4] Jesus is not a man who does the transcendent God an injustice by talking about him in limited human terms. He is God incarnate who reveals himself by entering limited human terms and turning them upside down. In meeting Jesus, we are meeting God.

> You have opened to us the Scriptures, O Christ,
> And you have made yourself known in the breaking of the bread.
> Abide with us, we pray,
> that, blessed by your royal presence,
> we may walk with you
> all the days of our life,
> and at its end behold you
> in the glory of the eternal Trinity,
> one God for ever and ever,
> Amen.

Notes

1 A meeting with Jesus

1 For a discussion of the need to be vindicated by the return of Jesus see Meeks, W. A. (1982) *The First Urban Christians*. New Haven, Conn.: Yale University Press, pp. 171–80. On the delay or otherwise of the return of Jesus, see the discussion in Rowland, C. C. (2002) *Christian Origins: The setting and character of the most important messianic sect of Judaism*. London: SPCK, pp. 287–93.

2 Parkes, C. M. (1972/1988) *Bereavement: Studies of grief in adult life*. Harmondsworth: Penguin, pp. 75–6.

3 Barton, J. (1997) *The Spirit and the Letter*. London: SPCK.

4 Burridge, R. (1992) 'What are the Gospels? A comparison with Graeco-Roman biography'. *Society for New Testament Studies Monograph Series 70*, Cambridge: Cambridge University Press.

5 The Gospel of Thomas appears to have been written in Greek in the second century AD, though most of it is known to us only in a later Coptic translation. It consists of 114 'sayings' of Jesus, many of which have parallels in the four canonical Gospels. However, the Gospel of Thomas contains no narrative whatsoever – it is merely a collection of sayings.

6 Brown, D. (2004) *The Da Vinci Code*. London: Corgi.

7 Williams, R. (1989) 'Does it make sense to speak of pre-Nicene orthodoxy?' In Williams, R. (ed.), *The Making of Orthodoxy: Essays in honour of Henry Chadwick*. Cambridge: Cambridge University Press, pp. 15–16.

8 Dunn, J. D. G. (2003) *Jesus Remembered*. Grand Rapids, Mich.: Eerdmans, p. 893.

9 Conzelmann, H. (1960) *The Theology of St Luke*. London: Faber & Faber, p. 100.

2 Drawing near

1 Moessner, D. (1989) *The Lord of the Banquet*. Minneapolis, Minn.: Fortress Press.

2 Crossan, J. D. (1994) *Jesus: A revolutionary biography*. San Francisco, Calif.: HarperSanFrancisco; (1991) *The historical Jesus*. San Francisco, Calif.: HarperSanFrancisco.
3 Lewis, C. S. (1950/1959) *The Lion, the Witch and the Wardrobe*. Harmondsworth: Puffin, pp. 165–6.
4 Hurley, S. (1998) *Consciousness in Action*. Cambridge, Mass.: Harvard University Press, pp. 403–04.
5 *qādôsh* (holy) and *pārush* (separated). The name 'Pharisee' is thought to be derived from *pārush*. See Bowker, J. (1973) *Jesus and the Pharisees*. Cambridge: Cambridge University Press, pp. 163, 164.

3 The heart of God

1 Crossan, J. D. (1980) *Cliffs of Fall: Paradox and polyvalence in the parables of Jesus*. New York: Seabury Press, p. 14.
2 Smith, P., Cowie, H. and Blades, M. (2003) *Understanding Children's Development*. Oxford: Blackwell. See Chapter 12 for a clear and balanced account of Piaget's theories and some primary references. See also Berryman, J. (1991) *Godly Play*. San Francisco, Calif.: HarperSanFrancisco, especially Chapter 7, for an excellent account of the way paradox can 'bind' our experience to God.
3 Kuhn, T. (1970) *The Structure of Scientific Revolutions*. Chicago, Ill.: University of Chicago Press.
4 '... paradox is not a dominant characteristic of the Pharisaic-rabbinic sayings ... as to such similitudes as ... lost sheep/lost coin ... prodigal son, unjust steward ... we have nothing of the same sort.' Neusner, J. (1971) *The Rabbinic Traditions about the Pharisees Before 70*. Leiden: Brill, p. 376.
5 Pargament, K. (1997) *The Psychology of Religion and Coping: Theory, practice and research*. New York: Guilford, p. 154.
6 Dodd, C. H. (1961) *The Parables of the Kingdom*. London: Fontana, p. 16.
7 McFague, S. (1985) *Metaphorical Theology: Models of God in religious language*. Philadelphia, Pa.: Fortress. This book draws attention to the two-edged nature of metaphor and the dangers of pressing images too far. For a more philosophical approach see Soskice, J. M. (1985) *Metaphor and Religious Language*. Oxford: Clarendon Press.
8 Panksepp, J. (1998) *Affective Neuroscience: The foundations of human and animal emotions*. Oxford: Oxford University Press.

4 The searching woman and the lost coin

1 LaHurd, C. S. (2002) 'Re-viewing Luke 15 with Arab Christian women'. In A. Levine (ed.) *A Feminist Companion to Luke*. Sheffield: Continuum, pp. 246–68.

2 Seim, T. K. (1994) *The Double Message: Patterns of gender in Luke–Acts*. Edinburgh: T & T Clark, pp. 143–4.

3 Tosefta Berakhot 6:8.

4 Archaeological evidence indicates that the manger is most likely to have been a *stone* feeding trough located inside the house. There is thus a physical resemblance to a tomb hewn from rock. For a detailed discussion see Bailey, K. (1979) 'The manger and the inn: The cultural background of Luke 2.7'. *Theological Review 2*, 33–44.

5 See note 7 Chapter 2. See also Salter, M. and Ainsworth, M. (1991) 'Attachments and other affectional bonds across the life cycle'. In C. M. Parkes, J. Stevenson-Hinde and P. Marris (eds) *Attachment Across the Life Cycle*. London: Routledge, pp. 33–51. See also McGrath, J. and McGrath, A. (2001) *Self-esteem: The cross and Christian confidence*. Leicester: Inter-Varsity Press, pp. 62–70.

6 Panksepp, J. (1998) *Affective Neuroscience: The Foundations of Human and Animal Emotions*. Oxford: Oxford University Press, Chapter 13.

7 Moltmann, J. (1981) 'The motherly Father: Is Trinitarian patri-passianism replacing theological patriarchalism?' *International Journal for Theology* 143, 51–6. Moltmann is the best known of a number of twentieth-century thinkers who have explored the theologically controversial notion of divine suffering. He argues that through the incarnation God the Son suffers alongside his people, and at the hands of his people, and God the Father suffers at the betrayal and death of his Son. The essence of this divine suffering is bereavement or separation distress. In this context Moltmann reflects on the figure of Mary, the *Pietà*, so often depicted in art. For further consideration of the *Pietà* see Greeley, A. (1977) *The Mary Myth*. New York: Seabury, Chapter 8. For a full discussion of the theology of divine suffering see Fiddes, P. (1992) *The Creative Suffering of God*. New York: Oxford University Press.

8 Janoff-Bulman, R. and McPherson Frantz, C. (1997) 'The impact of trauma on meaning: From meaningless world to meaningful life'. In M. Power and C. Brewin (eds) *The Transformation of Meaning in Psychological Therapies*. Chichester: Wiley, pp. 91–106.

9 For a discussion of sense-making in the context of health conditions in relation to the Babylonian exile see McGrath, J. (2004) 'Beyond restoration to transformation: Positive outcomes in the rehabilitation of acquired brain injury'. *Clinical Rehabilitation 18*, 767–75.

10 For example Lewis, C. S. (1955) *Surprised by Joy*. London: Geoffrey Bles, pp. 199, 214.

5 The lost son

1 Bailey, Kenneth (1980) *Through Peasant Eyes*. Grand Rapids, Mich.: Eerdmans.

2 Freud, Sigmund (1908) *Character and anal eroticism*. Charakter und Analerotik. Gesamelte Werke 5, 261 or Gesamelte Schriften 7, 203.

3 Douglas, Mary (1966) *Purity and Danger*. London: Routledge & Kegan Paul.

4 Lazarus, R. and Folkman, S. (1984) *Stress, Appraisal, and Coping*. New York: Springer.

5 Janoff-Bulman, R. (1992) *Shattered Assumptions: Towards a new psychology of trauma*. New York: The Free Press.

6 Pargament, K. (1997) *The Psychology and Religion of Coping: Theory, practice and research*. New York, Guilford, 154.4.

7 Ajzen, I. and Fishbein, M. (1980) *Understanding Attitudes and Predicting Social Behaviour*. Englewood Cliffs, N.J.: Prentice Hall, p. 5.

8 St Augustine, *Confessions*, translated by Chadwick, H. (1991) Oxford: Oxford University Press, X.29, 30, 35. Book X on memory, note especially X.27 on the story of the woman and the lost coin.

9 Sheldon, K. (2001) 'The self-concordance model of healthy goal-striving: When personal goals correctly represent the person'. In P. Schmuck and K. Sheldon (eds) *Life Goals and Well-Being: Towards a positive psychology of human striving*. Seattle, Wash.: Hogrefe & Huber.

6 The meeting

1 McGrath, J. and McGrath, A. (2001) *Self-esteem: The cross and Christian confidence*. Leicester: Inter-Varsity Press, pp. 68–9, 137–8.

2 Walker, R. M. (2000) *Politically Correct Parables*. London: Fount, pp. 13, 15.

3 Vanstone, W. H. (1982) *The Stature of Waiting*. London: Darton, Longman & Todd.

4 Bailey, Kenneth (1980) *Through Peasant Eyes*. Grand Rapids, Mich.: Eerdmans, p. 181.

5 La Hurd, C. S. (2000) 'Re-viewing Luke 15 with Arab Christian women'. In Levine, A. (ed.) *A feminist companion to Luke*. Sheffield, Continuum, pp. 246–68.

6 Bauman, Z. (1993) *Postmodern ethics*. Oxford: Blackwell, pp. 60, 61.

7 Levinas, E. (1981) *Otherwise than being*. London: Nijhoff, p. 82.

8 Volf, M. (1996) *Exclusion and embrace*. Nashville, Tenn.: Abingdon Press, Chapter 3.

9 Where a healing forms the backdrop to an account of a debate about the Sabbath, for instance Luke 13.10ff. and John 9, its description is abbreviated and this pattern is not evident in the text.

10 Wiebe, P. (1997) *Visions of Jesus*. New York: Oxford University Press.

11 Nouwen, H. (1992) *The Prodigal Son*. London: Darton, Longman & Todd, p. 13.

12 Lewis, C. S. (1955) *Surprised by Joy*. London: Geoffrey Bles. See pp. 158 and 207 on remembering, pp. 139, 205 on the sense of yielding and surrender, pp. 211–12, 215 on the image of removing restrictive clothing to become one's true self, pp. 214–17, 222–3 on the move from an embrace of theism to the personal knowing of Christ.

7 Envy and forgiveness

1 Averill, J. (1982) *Anger and Aggression: An essay on emotion*. New York: Springer-Verlag.

2 Sulloway, F. (1996) *Born to Rebel: Birth order, family dynamics, and creative lives*. New York: Pantheon.

3 James, W. (1896) *The Will to Believe*. New York: Longmans, Green. Erikson, E. (1980) *Identity and the Life Cycle*. New York: Norton.

4 A similar attitude perhaps lies beneath the first-century synagogue prayer that praises the God 'who did not make me a Gentile', 'who did not make me a slave' and 'who did not make me a woman'. (See note 3, Chapter 4.)

5 Schwartz, B. (2004) *The Paradox of Choice: When more means less.* New York: HarperCollins.

6 Nouwen, H. (1992) *The Prodigal Son.* London: Darton, Longman & Todd, p. 18.

7 See McGrath, J. and McGrath, A. (2001) *Self-esteem: The cross and Christian confidence.* Leicester: Inter-Varsity Press, for full discussion.

8 Feinberg, M., Neiderhiser, J., Simmens, S., Reiss, D. and Hetherington, E. (2000) 'Sibling comparison of differential parental treatment in adolescence: Gender, self-esteem, and emotionality as mediators of the parenting-adjustment association'. *Child Development* 71, 1611–28.

9 George and Weedon Grossmith (1892) *Diary of a Nobody.* London: Arrowsmith, pp. 49, 51.

10 Thorensen, C., Luskin, F. and Harris, A. (1998) 'Coronary heart disease: A psychosocial perspective on intervention'. In S. Royjroemer, S. Robinson and C. Carmin (eds) *The emerging role of counselling psychology in health care.* New York: Norton, pp. 94–136; Worthington, E., Sandage, S. and Berry, J. (2000) 'Group interventions to promote forgiveness: What researchers and clinicians ought to know'. In M. McCullough, K. Pargament and C. Thoresen (eds) *Forgiveness: Theory, research and practice.* New York: Guilford, pp. 228–53; Maltby, J., Macaskill, A. and Day, L. (2001) 'Failure to forgive self and others: A replication and extension of the relationship between forgiveness, personality, social desirability and general health'. *Personality and Individual Differences* 30, 881–5.

11 Enright, R. and Coyle, C. (1998) 'Researching the process model of forgiveness within psychological interventions'. In E. J. Worthington (ed.) *Dimensions of forgiveness,* Radnor, Pa.: Templeton Foundation Press, pp. 139–61.

8 Praiseworthy pragmatism

1 Bailey, K. B. (1983) *Poet and Peasant and Through Peasant Eyes.* Grand Rapids, Mich.: Eerdmans, pp. 101–2.

2 Derret, D. M. (1970) *Law in the New Testament.* London: Darton, Longman & Todd, p. 48ff.

3 Smith, B. (1937) *Parables of the Synoptic Gospels.* Cambridge: Cambridge University Press.

4 Psychologies that suggest the operation of more sinister unconscious or repressed agendas tend to be based on pathological clinical cases rather than more representative examples of human activity. See Wilson, T. (2002) *Strangers to Ourselves*. Cambridge, Mass.: Belknap Press; Brewin, C. and Andrews, B. (2000) 'What did Freud get right?' *The Psychologist* 13, 605–7.

5 See Peace, R. (1999) *Conversion in the New Testament*. Grand Rapids, Mich.: Eerdmans, for a critical study.

6 Perhaps surprisingly, there is still much scholarly debate over the nature and identity of the Pharisees. A good place to start is Saldarini, A. J. (2001) *Pharisees, Scribes and Sadducees in Palestinian Society*. Grand Rapids, Mich.: Eerdmans.

9 The window of opportunity

1 Neusner, J., Scott Green, W. and Fredrichs, E. (1987) *Judaisms and Their Messiahs at the Turn of the Christian Era*. Cambridge: Cambridge University Press.

2 See, for example, Josephus, *Antiquities* 18.23 and *Jewish War* 2.433.

3 Prochaska, J. and Diclemente, C. (1983) 'Stages and process of self-change of smoking: Towards an integrative model of change'. *Journal of Consulting & Clinical Psychology* 51, 390–5.

4 Curtis Mayfield, 1964.

10 Meeting Jesus

1 Bauckham, R. (2002) *Gospel Women*. Grand Rapids, Mich.: Eerdmans, p. 183.

2 Dix, G. (1945) *The Shape of the Liturgy*. Westminster: Dacre Press.

3 Wiebe, P. (1997) *Visions of Jesus*. New York: Oxford University Press. In this respect it was very different from the usual experience of bereaved people, whose attention is so taken up with the person they have lost that everything reminds them of the loved one, who may also appear to them in dreams or hallucinations.

4 Brunner, E. (1964) *Truth as Encounter*. London: SCM Press, p. 24.

Further reading

Specific points can be followed up in the notes for each chapter. The following are suggestions for the reader who wants to read around some of the themes in this book.

Historical and political background

Borg, M. (1998) *Conflict, Holiness, and Politics in the Teaching of Jesus.* Harrisburg, Pennsylvania: Trinity Press.

Josephus, Flavius *The Antiquities of the Jews.* Various translations available.

Myers, C. (1988) *Binding the Strong Man: A political reading of Mark's story of Jesus.* Maryknoll, New York: Orbis Books.

Sanders, E. P. (1993) *The Historical Figure of Jesus.* London: Penguin.

Theissen, G. and Merz, A. (1998). *The Historical Jesus.* London: SCM Press.

Women's issues and feminist approaches to the Bible

For two different approaches to wisdom, see Dunn, J. (1989) *Christology in the Making.* London: SCM Press, Chapter 6, pp. 163–212. Also, Schüssler Fiorenza, E. (1995*) Jesus: Miriam's Child, Sophia's Prophet.* London: SCM Press, Chapter 5, pp. 131–55.

Levine, A. (2002) *A Feminist Companion to Luke.* Sheffield: Continuum.

Taylor Gench, F. (2004) *Back to the well: Women's encounters with Jesus in the Gospels.* Louisville, Ky: Westminster/John Knox Press.

Trauma and spirituality

Collicutt McGrath, J. (2006) 'Post-traumatic Growth and the Origins of Early Christianity.' *Mental Health, Religion and Culture 9,* 291–306.

Tedeschi, R. and Calhoun, L. (1995) *Trauma and Transformation: Growing in the aftermath of suffering.* Thousand Oaks, Calif.: Sage.

Goals, well-being, and spirituality

Brunstein, J., Schultheiss, O., and Graessman, R. (1998) 'Personal goals and emotional well-being: The moderating role of motive dispositions.' *Journal of Personality and Social Psychology 75,* 494–508.

Emmons, R. (1999) *The Psychology of Ultimate Concerns.* New York: Guilford.

Psychological approaches to transforming experiences

James, W. (1902) *The Varieties of Religious Experience*. London: Penguin (1982). Lectures 9 and 10.

Loder, J. (1989) *The Transforming Moment*. Colorado Springs, Colo.: Helmers & Howard, especially pp. 1–33.

Prochasla, J. and Norcross, J. *Systems of Psychotherapy: A transtheoretical analysis*. Pacific Grove, Calif.: Brooks/Cole, especially pp. 1–26, 479–509.

Forgiveness

Holloway, R. (2002) *On Forgiveness: How can we forgive the unforgivable?* Edinburgh: Canongate Books.

Monbourquette, J. (2000) *How to Forgive*. London: Darton, Longman & Todd/Novalis.

Watts, F. and Gulliford, L. (2004) *Forgiveness in Context: Theology and psychology in creative dialogue*. London: Continuum.

Parables

Bailey, Kenneth E. (1983) *Poet and Peasant and Through Peasant Eyes* (Combined edition). Grand Rapids, Mich.: Eerdmans.

Longenecker, Richard N. (2000) *The Challenge of Jesus' Parables*, *McMaster New Testament Studies*. Grand Rapids, Mich.: Eerdmans.

Wenham, David (1989) *The Parables of Jesus, Jesus Library*. London: Hodder & Stoughton.

The dishonest manager

For a vivid account of the turning of a dishonest man, see Aitken, J. (2000) *Pride and Perjury*. London: HarperCollins.

Derret, D. M. (1961) 'Fresh light on St. Luke XV.I: The parable of the unjust steward'. *New Testament Studies* 7, 198–219.

Williams, R. (2004) *Anglican Identities*. London: Darton, Longman & Todd, pp. 9–23.

Eschatology

Alison, J. (1997) *Living in the End Times: The last things re-imagined*. London: SPCK.

Chaos theory

Gleick, J. (1988) *Chaos: Making a new science*. Penguin, London.

The journal *Nonlinear Dynamics, Psychology, and Life Sciences* published by Springer Netherlands is also useful.